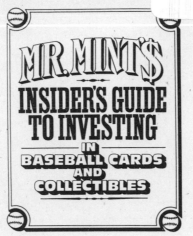

MR. MINT'$
INSIDER'S GUIDE TO INVESTING
IN BASEBALL CARDS AND COLLECTIBLES

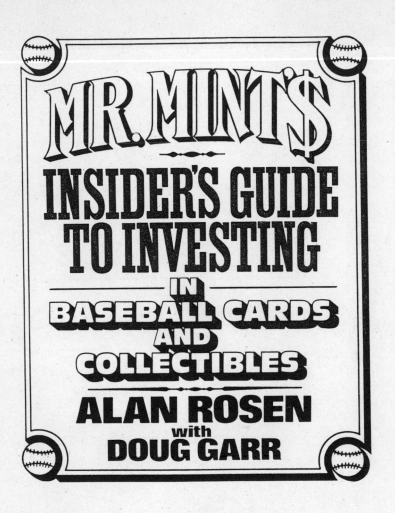

MR. MINT$

INSIDER'S GUIDE TO INVESTING
IN BASEBALL CARDS AND COLLECTIBLES

ALAN ROSEN
with DOUG GARR

WARNER BOOKS

A Time Warner Company

Warner Books, Inc., 666 Fifth Avenue, New York, NY 10103

W A Time Warner Company

Printed in the United States of America
First printing: July 1991
10 9 8 7 6 5 4 3 2 1

Library of Congress Cataloging-in-Publication Data

Rosen, Alan, 1946–
    Mr. Mint's insider's guide to investing in baseball cards and
collectibles / Alan Rosen with Doug Garr.
      p. cm.
    Includes bibliographical references.
    ISBN 0-446-39252-9
    1. Baseball cards—Collectors and collecting—United States.
I. Garr, Doug.
GV875.3.R67   1991
769′.49796357′0973—dc20   91-2270
                                             CIP

Book design by Giorgetta Bell McRee
Cover design by Don Puckey
Cover photo by Theo Westenberger, Sygma

To
Marnee, Jennie,
and Blake

CONTENTS

ACKNOWLEDGMENTS

The genesis of any book is often complicated, but readers might be interested to know that this investor's guide book had decidedly simple origins. I met Doug Garr early in 1990 on a rainy winter evening when he drove out to my home in Montvale, New Jersey, to do an interview with me. On assignment for *BusinessWeek*'s "Access," a quarterly investment supplement for the magazine's subscribers, Garr was writing a trends piece about the future of baseball cards.

I talked steadily into his tape recorder until we exhausted his supply of tape. I showed him around my basement; and his eyes dripped with envy when I let him hold Eddie Collins' bat and Cal Ripken, Jr.'s, spikes. He snickered a little when he saw a picture of Reggie Jackson autographed to me and inscribed, "The Mr. October of Baseball Cards." Wayne Miller, a fellow dealer and friend, had added, "The Straw that Stirs the Drink." Later, Garr said I reminded him of Dizzy Dean, a baseball player who was known to brag all the time about how good he was. The great St. Louis pitcher, of course, had the talent to back up what he said. Well, the closest I came to being Dizzy Dean was when I pitched in the Little League.

By the time it was early morning, Garr suggested we do a book together. He had rightly noted that whereas there were a hundred books on how to invest in real estate and in the stock market, there was virtually nothing about how to buy a rare baseball card. Someone else once suggested I do an investment book, but the idea never took hold. I thought Garr was just flattering me, too.

We'd known each other only five or six hours, but after all, we had a few major things in common. We were both born in the Bronx, and we were both die-hard Yankees fans. And we thought today's players couldn't carry the jocks of the guys we saw when we were kids in the 1950s. It was enough of a bond to produce this book. Garr has since become a collector again, slyly accumulating a few thousand cards while he translated my thoughts onto paper. Mostly, he followed my advice.

Several people contributed their time and expertise in the research for this book, and this is the appropriate spot to express my appreciation. I'd like to thank Bob Schmierer of the Eastern Pennsylvania Sports Collectors Club. Bob is as well versed as anyone with the history of the hobby and is the promotor of the well-known Willow Grove shows. He made himself available to Garr while he was busy promoting his shows.

Over the years I've worked very closely with a few selective dealers. I truly feel without their friendship, trust, and guidance, this book never would have happened. Barry Halper of Livingston, New Jersey, John Broggi of Highland Park, New Jersey, Joseph Esposito of Thornwood, New York, Paul Lewicki of Wyckoff, New Jersey, Steve Reeves of Kensington, Maryland, Rick Starks of Erie, Pennslyvania, Bill Hongach of Brooklyn, New York, Bill Mastro of Palos Park, Illinois. My right-hand man, Glenn Stuart, who for years has taken my abuse with a smile. To him I say thank you.

There are a host of others who have contributed to my success, and I would like to thank them also. Aubrey and Linda Shoemaker, Bruce Paynter, Roger "the Dodger" Hecht, James Copeland, Ron Oser, Barry Sanders, Phil and Joan Spector, Jim

Hawkins, the great *Sports Collectors Digest* staff, Mike Berkus, Jack Petruzelli, Jonathan Gallen, Wayne Tenenbaum, J.W. Jones, and of course Bertha and Louis, Sandra and Larry Alder. Also, there were undoubtedly dozens of other collectors, hobbyists, and dealers who helped. If I've forgotten you, forgive my faulty memory.

Jim Frost, late of Warner, was the editor who acquired the book, and we're thankful for his prescience. Charlie Conrad, no stranger to the world of pricey baseball cards, inherited Frost's early enthusiasm for the manuscript and patiently helped us shape it for publication. Thanks, too, to our agent, Barbara Lowenstein. Babs knows books.

Lastly, I'd like to thank my wife, Marnee, a baseball card widow if there ever was one, who puts up with my long weekends away at card shows. I can't forget to express my gratitude to another woman, Meg Perlman, who is married to Garr. She provided support and encouragement during the research and writing.

—Alan Rosen
October 1990

AUTHOR'S NOTE

This book has been prepared to be of value to both the neophyte collector/investor and the seasoned veteran. Perhaps, too, even a few smarmy teenagers who've been wheeling and dealing Ryne Sandberg and Jose Canseco cards will also learn a few lessons about the often volatile and capricious world of baseball cards and collectibles.

Only one disclaimer: This is not intended to be a price guide in any way. Many other publishers purvey this kind of information in books, magazines, and newspapers. I refer to prices in this book only to illustrate certain points, and not to suggest how much to pay for cards or memorabilia. By the time you're reading this, the prices will be woefully outdated, one way or the other.

—A.R.

INTRODUCTION

In an earlier, far less successful professional life, I sold jewelry, antiques, sewing machines, refrigerators, furs, insurance, and photocopiers. I sold the copy machines door-to-door, and mostly suffered rejection. I had to haul a lot of machines around to eke out a decent living. I was unhappy, struggling, and disillusioned. Uneducated (I received a high school equivalency diploma but had no college credits), I was at least smart enough to realize I was never going to make the Swedish Academy's short list for the Nobel Prize in Economics.

Then, suddenly, I chucked everything to take a shot at earning a living doing something I loved. I became a baseball card dealer. I will never forget the day I knew I'd make it. I borrowed every penny my mother-in-law had, to buy a bunch of old Turkey Red, T-205, and T-206 cards. I laid out $12,000 in cash in the morning. That evening, I drove from my tiny apartment in Hackensack, New Jersey, to a dealer's home in Maryland and sold them for $28,500. I'd earned $16,500 in one day. (Those cards would easily bring $500,000 in today's market, incidentally.) I had to sell an awful lot of photocopiers to make that kind of money.

I first became a full-time baseball card and collectible dealer at the beginning of the 1980s, when there were very few people who could make a living doing nothing else but buying and selling cards. So I had an edge. I knew I could be more aggressive and knowledgeable than the guy who only bought and sold cards after work and on weekends.

The other thing I noticed when I first began dealing cards was that they weren't very respectable in terms of the public at large. They were respectable only to kids. (It took years before I was able to tell my banker what I really did for a living. To him I was a "collectibles" dealer and not a baseball card salesman.) They were low-ranking on the food chain of collectibles, well below antiques, rare coins, and stamps. I knew the only way to change this was getting the hobby in print. The way to do this was by making big deals and getting them noticed. Card collecting was growing by huge leaps, the market was hyperactive.

I decided to trade on two ideas. One, I knew that most dealers didn't have a lot of capital. They scraped together enough money and rounded up partners when they attempted to buy large collections. No bank was going to lend them money to buy baseball cards. I knew if I could work my operating capital up to a high enough level, I could outbid my competitors. Two, I also knew that there were a lot of bad-condition cards around and very little top-quality stuff. I'd deal only in high-grade merchandise, and I'd brag about it whenever I could.

Once my business began to grow, I started carrying a briefcase with $150,000 in cash to card shows, and I made certain that plenty of spectators were around when I made a big deal. This admittedly show-off way of transacting business, as well as my penchant for latching onto great-looking old cards, helped to earn my sobriquet, "Mr. Mint."

The bottom line is that the Mint Man has most of the cash, and he knows who has the biggest collections. There are a few dealers who know more about cards than I do, and when people decide to sell out, I have primed them to at least consider me a top—if not the top—broker and buyer in the business.

When Stan Martucci, who owned a concession across the street from Yankee Stadium, wanted to sell his card collection, he didn't think twice to consider anyone else. He called me one day and said, "Are you the hotshot guy I've been reading about? Mr. Mint, I want you over at my house next week, on Wednesday. Bring about $45,000 with you." At the time, I still needed a partner, and I called Rick Starks, who was a dealer before I was, and we each put up about $25,000. We bought a considerable number of Martucci's cards and threw a little card party for dealers. We realized a $25,000 profit for about three days' effort.

In the 1980s, I made a number of big buys, or "finds," which I made sure to boast about in my ads. I'll never forget being flabbergasted when I went to the home of the son of a truck driver in Lowell, Massachusetts. The man's dad had worked for the distributor of Topps cards in the 1950s. There were bricks of gem mint 1952s; dozens of perfect Mantles, Robinsons, Campanellas, Mays cards. I brought $100,000 with me. I left with all the cards and barely enough money to buy gas to get home. Of course, I had buyer's remorse. I wondered if I was slightly insane in exchanging all that cash for pieces of cardboard. But in the next month, I made well over $100,000.

When those cards come on the market today, they're often advertised as coming from the "Mr. Mint find."

Today, as one of the nation's biggest and most visible baseball card dealers, my marketing techniques have been criticized quite a bit. I've been accused of being a publicity monger, ambitious, and arrogant. The sum of these three indiscretions adds up to my projecting an image that was allegedly "bad for the hobby." Let me say right away that the first three accusations may be true; perhaps I'm occasionally guilty of bad manners. But the fourth one is not. (Most of my colleagues' gripes are uttered out of jealousy or envy).

Somehow, negative criticism has a way of recycling itself in a positive way. A dealer who disapproves of my bluster and aggressive marketing techniques, and admittedly doesn't like me very much, put it this way: "In the long run, what Rosen does is promote cards for all of us. We're all recipients, in a way, of his publicity efforts. His enthusiasm and hard work trickle down into more business for the rest of us." It's one of the nicest compliments I've ever received.

There is a certain degree of truth to the fact that dealers like myself have changed the business, or, to put it more bluntly, "destroyed the hobby." I've heard it so much that I've stopped trying to rebut it. It's like saying today's ball players' demands for huge salaries have ruined the game. Critics have been saying that since the turn of the century. It's just not true. Baseball cards grew up, that's all. Yes, the hobby was transmogrified into a business, seemingly overnight. Everyone agrees about that. What the old-timers won't accept is that this change is irrevocable. There's no going back to the days of casual trading. Cards are big business, and they're trying to ignore this fact.

My personal taste for baseball card definitions goes something like this. The words *industry* and *business* are the umbrella terms for anything marketable under baseball the sport, from old cards to Houston Astros coffee mugs. *Hobby* refers to the part of the business where people who buy cards and collectibles are in it strictly, or primarily, for enjoyment. There are all kinds of *collectors,* and they fall under the rubric of hobbyists and other terms, but this is more complicated, and I'll explain their distinct characteristics later in the book. It is hoped that you're reading this book because you're mainly interested in learning more about cards to make money investing—by buying and selling—cards and collectibles. If all you're interested in is saving the cards forever, then you'll likely find this book useful, anyway. But if you just want to squirrel away cheap cards in the attic, you don't necessarily need my advice—or anyone else's, for that matter.

As a dealer, I'm still a strong believer in the hobby. I'm all for kids buying new-season issues and flipping and trading them. (Collectors who still prefer to spend their weekends trading their common player cards worth 10 cents apiece with their friends can still call it a hobby, by the way.) But the others who are shelling out thousands of dollars for collections prefer to think of baseball cards as a business. And they'd rather consider themselves as investors first and collectors second. Or, if they want to consider themselves primarily collectors, they want to collect with the word "investment" not very far from their minds. Yes, they enjoy owning cards, but they'd like to make a profit when they eventually sell them.

So, in the following pages, I'll reveal the secrets of my trade. I'll offer information that the typical dealer doesn't necessarily want you to know. The book will be something of a reintroduction for all of you who haven't touched a card since you were a kid. But more important, it will be a crash course in investing.

Yes, I can hear my critics now. Rosen, who has already ruined the hobby, is about to bury it with the publication of this book. But it's what I know, and it's an honest view.

In sum, I'll take all the heat. I haven't touched a photocopier in years.

BASEBALL CARDS
ARE FOREVER

When I was an adolescent, I was just like any other kid who collected baseball cards. They were conveniently sized pieces of cardboard that fit in your pants pockets. Looking back, assessing their value from a 12-year-old's perspective poses a vexing question. Were they worth less than the penny apiece we paid, or were they priceless? The answer is both. It depended on the particular player's card and your mood on a given day.

Many years after I stopped collecting cards as a kid, I decided to attend a baseball card show. I had seen an ad in the newspaper, and it piqued me. When I strolled into my first show in Parsippany, New Jersey, in 1978, there were 300 tables full of baseball cards beckoning. At the time, I had no idea what kind of an impact it would have on my life. There, under so many glass cases, were the ghosts of heroes past. Anson and Lajoie, Mays and Mize and Mantle, Ruth and Robinson, DiMaggio, Gehrig. Players who were legends, and players who had maybe a single season of glory. Great or near great, or merely a guy who filled in the lineup card for a star, they were all somehow pieces of the puzzle that revealed the American past. A short walk through the show provided a history lesson of the mustachioed men who played the game a century ago in striped caps and heavy flannel shirts with collars.

I was stunned. It was almost something spiritual, thinking once again about my childhood role models. That's what got me thinking about starting to collect again. For others, the response is less cerebral. It might even be described as Pavlovian. They might notice a pack of current Topps cards and the slab of bubble gum, which has gotten smaller and more brittle over the years since I was a kid but still miraculously possesses that same seductive, sugary scent. Others remember flipping and trading the cards, or attaching them to the frame of their bikes with clothespins, so they flicked against the spokes, simulating the sound of a loud motorcycle. And perhaps some recall not talking to their best buddy because he refused to trade a Moose Skowron double for a Hank Bauer.

What truly hooked me at that Parsippany show was the 1953 Mickey Mantle card, his second-year Topps card, #82. I was brought up in the Bronx, and there were few baseball fans in the 1950s from that borough whose allegiance wasn't firmly pledged to the Bombers in pinstripes. I began daydreaming about all the days that I spent inside Yankee Stadium, charting my boyhood hero. My father, who was a press photographer, actually took a picture of me as a boy with Mantle on the field.

When I saw that card, something happened. It all came back, like a summer deluge, my youth, the dirt and the smudges of Little League, the capricious dreams of life on the road in the big leagues. I'd had that Mickey Mantle card when I was a kid (a refrain that dealers hear so often at card shows, it rolls their eyeballs). It was my favorite card. I remembered how I shoveled snow to save money for candy store binges; as soon as I earned $1.20, I bought 24 packs of cards. Hoping for a Mantle. Praying.

Well, the 1953 Mantle card I spied in 1978 wasn't perfect—it showed some wear—but I didn't care that it was handled a bit. Somebody out there, maybe a half dozen previous owners, had marveled over the same reproduction of the Mick's youthful face, full of promise of the brilliant career that lay ahead. It gave me the same glow. I checked the price guides at the time. The card was booking for $95, but I paid $120, which wasn't all that unusual. The card was both scarce and in great demand. (The only thing that might seem a bit out of whack was that someone was willing to pay $120 for something that cost only a penny 25 years earlier.) But I'd been a coin collector, and like most kids, I understood that people commonly paid more for things that were in great demand and were fairly scarce. I put the Mantle card in a plastic holder and displayed it on my desk, like other businessmen did with photos of their children. Looking back 12 years, I guess I was trying to recapture a misspent youth. A cliché, perhaps, but one I can feel good thinking about.

Only now, of course, do I know enough to recall that I really didn't know what I was doing when I bought that Mantle card. In the late 1970s, there were very few full-time professional dealers, and the market (if you can call it one) was in its nascency. In fact, baseball card collecting was still more of a hobby than a business, as it is today.

Things have changed rapidly in the last dozen years. Baseball cards and related items have gained the respectability normally associated with the word "collectible." Like me, those born during World War II, the first generation of baby boomers, had children of their own who became entranced by their own diamond stars—Brett, Rose, Schmidt, Carlton, Jackson, Morgan, Seaver, and Ryan. This first generation took their kids to card shows at their kids' behest, and—surprise—they got involved again. Baseball cards are like Disney World in this respect. Parents may look forward to the age when their kids can allow them to become kids again.

The last decade saw an unprecedented growth in baseball the game and baseball the card and collectible business. Major-league attendance is at an all-time high. National League expansion is all but a fait accompli. The question that remains is, merely, where will the new franchise (or franchises) be located? As this book went into production, there was talk of Denver, Tampa, or Buffalo being the newest city to host a team.

The last decade also saw tremendous gains in baseball card popularity. Part-time dabblers became full-time card dealers. A bunch of fellows in their 40s finally bagged their jobs as personnel directors and managers and devoted their entire attention to buying and selling baseball cards. The result was a nation of born-again fanatics.

Many of these new fans are what we dealers call the suits—the dentists, surgeons, and businessmen who now frequently parade through card shops and shows with big bankrolls looking for solid investments. They've gone to a few ball games, perhaps for the first time in years. They have a vague idea who some of the movers and shakers are strolling the infield in their tight-fitting cotton pullovers. They've read about their multimillion-dollar salaries—egads, Jose Canseco has better financials than Donald Trump these days!—and they've even stayed current by glancing at the prices of baseball cards in guidebooks. In fact, the weekly price guide listings of cards in the trade press are somewhat akin to the closing stock market prices printed every day in the nation's newspapers.

These new collectors are pouring money into cards, of course, and they're largely lured by the expectation of a profit. Their feeling is, why not diversify my portfolio? There's no real enjoyment involved with a CD or zero coupon bond, anyway. You may be one of those folks. No harm in that logic, as long as you're aware that when money is the sole or prime factor, you are an investor and not a collector. Perhaps the hobby/business needs both to survive and to thrive. Smart buyers must keep both "collection" and "investment" in mind.

In some ways, even the most cynical, old-fashioned dealers are secretly or openly glad there's a lot of new collector interest. Sure, there are always those fans who are more interested in what the latest price guide says about a recent acquisition than what piece of history the item actually represents. These buyers are easily able to shut out of the market the teenagers shopping for rookie cards with their summer job earnings. But the new collectors have caused the more expensive memorabilia aspect of the business—old uniforms, gloves, bats, balls, spikes, stadium seats, press pins, autographed pictures—to really take off. Back when I bought that Mantle card for $120, people thought I paid a lot of money for a baseball card, no matter how "valuable" it was deemed. Had someone predicted that someday a *current* player's rookie card would exceed $1,000, we all might have thought the idea was ridiculous. Yet Nolan Ryan's 1968 Topps card (which he shares with Jerry Koosman) was selling for $1,200 to $1,500 months *before* he tossed his sixth no-hitter in the 1990 season.

The market value of baseball cards, in general (and I emphasize "in general"), increased at an annual rate of 20 to 35 percent in the 1980s. That's quite an article of faith in little pieces of cardboard measuring only 2½ by 3½ inches (actually the very expensive, very old tobacco cards are even smaller). While a 20 to 35 percent return is encouraging, it reflects windfall profits on unexpected winners as well as some cards whose market value has fallen. But you must more closely analyze the 20 to 35 percent figure. It likely reflects the Major League Industrials Average—the blue chip cards only. It does not always account for flat-out duds, wildly speculative investments on more current merchandise. In an extensive analysis of the card market in 1988, *Money* magazine reported that rookie cards produced a compound annual rate of return of 42.5 percent in the 1980s, far outperforming corporate bonds, common stocks, Treasury bills, diamonds, gold, and silver. Of course, this does not mean that everyone who bought cards made money on every investment, any more than someone who has been successful in the stock market has nailed a winner in every pick.

I've often heard dealers and collectors say that anyone with even a pea brain could have made money buying and selling cards if they'd gotten involved early enough. Is it fair to say that had the average investor had the prescience to buy old cards in the early 1980s and wanted to sell them today, his rate of return would have been phenomenal? Yes. But the pea brain days are long over, and it's harder than ever to make careful, selective investments. Still, it can be done, and that's one of the reasons for this book. If you've decided to buy cards and other collectibles with the hope of average to high growth, then you can't just automatically assume everything you buy will increase by one-fifth to one-third, every year.

If it were that easy, you wouldn't need this book, nor would you need any advice at all.

I'm not going to dwell too much on the statistical profile of the collectors in the hobby, because there are many rough figures given, and it's impossible to count them, anyway. I've read that there are 1.5 million collectors of varying levels of involvement in the United States. There are some 10,000 dealers nationwide, someone else says. And the gross national product of baseball merchandise and memorabilia is somewhere between $150 million and $1 billion annually. Well, don't take any of it too literally. Ours is a cash business, and the vast majority of dealers are part-timers who work weekends and nights. It's enough to say there's a lot of people in cards and collectibles, and a lot of money is spent every day. Today, there are, of course, more players in the game. More people simply "know about" baseball cards.

Financial pundits have polled dealers and promoters of cards and have predicted that the 1990s won't see the same spectacular growth experienced in the 1980s. There will be a slight recession, say some, and others predict a "correction," and still other doomsayers see a bottoming out. A downturn would certainly be a natural reaction in a market that is as cyclical as any other. But my feeling is that if the market does drift downward, it will rebound to higher levels than before. I may sound like a Wall Street shill, but I sincerely think there are opportunities to be found in either an up or down market. As an aggressive buyer myself, I've often gone against the popular tidal waves. When people are selling in droves, I'm a buyer. And when people are hoarding—waiting for the market to get another jolt—I'm often a seller.

Although the industry is somewhat grown up, it is not sophisticated in many other ways. Perhaps the most glaring problem is the lack of professional dealer unity. There is not yet an organized trade association, even though there have been 11 national conventions. There is no single, central regulatory body, no built-in protection for buyers and collectors and speculators. Anyone who is new to the game should be aware of this deficiency (though there has been an ongoing effort to organize the dealer ranks over the past few years).

Many readers might think that the title of this chapter, "Baseball Cards Are Forever," reflects an unreasonably rosy view of the industry. It does not. The card market can be moody, to be sure, but so is the overall behavior of the beloved game itself. Before the 1989 season belatedly began, a young collector asked a dealer if he thought the owners' lockout would affect the delivery schedule of the new season's baseball cards. "Son," the dealer said, "there may not be baseball this year. But there will be baseball cards. I guarantee it."

By the time you read this, baseball's greatest singles hitter, Pete Rose, will have served five months in the slammer for income tax evasion. A major-league umpire was arrested and charged with shoplifting baseball cards. A San Luis Obispo man was bludgeoned to death during an attempted robbery of his son's card store. A large, already successful new card company, Upper Deck, was started a few seasons ago because a collector was angry at the number of bogus Don Mattingly cards that had flooded into the country's card shops.

Baseball isn't all halos. So what else is new? Naturally, everyone involved in the game is not an angel. But the game, somehow, elevates itself to some incomprehensible status. Thanks perhaps to some deity, baseball has its own indefinable inertia. It endures. It will outlast us all, despite strikes, penurious owners, unrealistically greedy players, lousy trades, earthquakes, injuries, assorted major- and minor-league transgressions, and other mayhem. Somehow, at least to me, baseball cards are truly forever, even if it's more difficult to spot a truly wonderful bargain. But if you follow my advice, and put a minimum amount of time into studying the marketplace, you'll find that you can make successful, lucrative investments.

STARTING OVER

Let's assume you just got off the phone with your mother, and she's delivered the dispiriting but not unexpected news: During one inspired spring cleaning, probably while you were off at college, she threw away all of your baseball cards. Those Thom McAn shoe boxes full of cards you collected when you were a kid and safely stored in the attic are now resting in the great baseball card graveyard, already recycled by nature into this year's crop of aspiring rookies.

As a former child hobbyist interested in becoming a serious collector/investor, this news is painful, but it need not be traumatic. First, you've got to remember that there is a market at all because of the wonderful moms of America who tossed their kids' cards in the trash can. It's mothers like yours who helped create the demand and put dealers like me in business. Second, as an adolescent, you likely conformed to the uniform spirit of collecting cards. When you bought them, like I did, you immediately began flipping and trading them when the bubble gum was still tough in your cheeks. You roughed them up in the playground because they were playthings and not commodities. If a young hopeful on your favorite team had a bad season, you did what George Steinbrenner and other impatient owners frequently do today. You traded the bum, or worse, ripped up his card.

Finally, if your mother hadn't eighty-sixed all your cards, someone else (even yourself) would have. Now, don't you feel better?

What am I getting at here? Simply, that the odds are that your once-hallowed collection of baseball cards probably wouldn't be worth much had it survived. The condition of the cards, which is so critical to their value, would have been noninvestment quality. What you once assumed to be good or excellent condition is just not very desirable or worthwhile from the strictly fiscal point of view.

Recently, a writer who had published a cogent, informative article for an airline magazine about the president of Topps cheerfully informed a friend that his mother saved all his cards. He wasn't particularly smug about it, but you could see he was pleased when he reeled off an inventory that included a dozen or so early 1960s Mantle, Mathews, Musial, and Aaron cards. He'd checked a price guide and was gratified to see that some of his cards had a book value of $250 to $300 each. However, when someone I know saw the cards, a familiar story emerged.

Even though they were carefully stored in plastic holders, almost every card had worn corners. They were like good, solid used cars. Hardly beat up, certainly in good working order, but nothing to show off at an antique or collectible show. It didn't take long for him to realize that his select group of 50 or 60 cards was worth probably only a couple of hundred dollars rather than the few thousand he'd hoped. But that's okay, because when he first stowed them away, he didn't expect them to ever be worth anything. He's still got the cards; he'll save them for his children or grandchildren to enjoy.

In a conventional investment guide, you might think the most obvious, basic advice to a beginning card collector would be: Don't buy any cards until you finish this book. Well, this isn't an ordinary advice book, and I think your urge to acquire something should immediately be satisfied. Most collectors buy first and learn later. I did, and there's no reason to suppose it's still a bad idea. But let's modifiy the standard homily a bit. Don't do anything rash; that is, don't make an unusually large purchase until you've finished the book and at least have a vague idea of what you're up against.

If you're serious about getting involved with collecting, I'm going to assume you're still something of a baseball fan. You should spend some time with the sports pages of your local paper (and also *USA Today,* which gives the best overall baseball coverage). Start reading the box scores again, ten minutes a day over coffee. You need not be obsessive about memorizing batting averages, but a healthy breeze through baseball statistics will help prepare you to analyze the careers of today's stars, even though I'm not going to recommend putting much money into "current players." This isn't like pork bellies futures, where to be successful you don't need to know a pig from a cow, though it's to your distinct advantage to know how the vagaries of the market affect the prices. In order to be a baseball card and memorabilia collector, trader, and investor, you've got to love the game more than you thought you ever could.

So, take a Saturday afternoon and forget about puttering in your basement or mowing the lawn. Off to the local baseball card shop. If you don't know where one is, check the Yellow Pages. If your community is so helplessly rural, you may have to look for the local coin dealer or comic book dealer. Many of these salesmen cross over into related memorabilia collecting. You never know where you'll find cards for sale. There's an antique dealer in Eastport, New York, whose son has taken a corner of the store and sells cards.

If you haven't seen a baseball card display at a supermarket in some time, then you're in for a rude surprise. There are now five companies who print pictures of major-league players on cardboard every season. They are Topps, Score, Fleer, Donruss, and Upper Deck. Only Topps includes a stick of gum. Okay, jump in. Take out a $10 bill and buy a couple of packs of each company's wares. If the store owner has any foresight at all, any hope of cultivating you as a long-term customer, he might even throw in a pack for free. But don't worry about it if he doesn't. This is merely a scouting expedition, a means for you to get back in touch with each company's products.

Open the packs and sift through the cards. Relax, there is scant chance that you are touching any card that will soon be worth more than the 4 or 5 cents you just paid.

MR. MINT'S MAXIM: *Learn how to handle the cards like a collector. You should be able to quickly shuffle through a pack of 15 or 17 cards without crimping the edges or nicking the corners. Sooner or later, you'll be holding a card worth several hundred dollars. And while you should be extremely careful with the valuable ones, you still must hold one to properly inspect it.*

So, other than feeling like a kid again, what is the first thing you noticed? The Topps, Score, and Donruss cards are printed on cheap cardboard, while the Fleer and Upper Decks are manufactured on slightly stiffer, better-quality stock. Fleer and Upper Decks have a stark white background, on both the front and the reverse. The Upper Decks are glossier than the others. The reverse also has a 2-centimeter-diameter hologram, which the company says makes it next to impossible to counterfeit. For this, Upper Deck charges a premium; its cards are typically double the retail price of the other four companies.

You've now faced your first problem, albeit a minor one. Which cards do you buy? The Upper Decks are certainly far and away more aesthetically pleasing than Upper Deck's competitors, but as an investment do they make any more sense than buying other companies' current cards? The answer is probably no. It doesn't make a difference. The future value of these cards hinges almost solely on what rookies are in the sets. And virtually nobody—not even the scout who signed him—knows whether a rookie phenom is Hall of Fame material while he's still a rookie.

There's another problem, too. If you're an ex–coin collector, or hoarded Lincoln pennies or Jefferson nickels as a child, then you understand mintage and circulation. If you wanted to know how many 1931-S Lincoln pennies were minted, you checked a guidebook and discovered the government made only 866,000. Since pennies are regularly minted in the tens of millions a year, you can easily assess the relative scarcity of any given penny.

But cards pose a much larger, frustrating challenge. All the companies except for Upper Deck fiercely guard the annual mintage and sales figures for their cards. (It's somewhat disappointing that Topps and Fleer follow this policy, because they're publicly traded companies. But their annual reports reveal only the financial information they're required to publish.) The reason is simple. By withholding this basic information from collectors and dealers, it is impossible for an investor and collector to gauge current (and more important, future) scarcity. Information gathered in the business revolving around print orders is almost always the result of guesswork and the dealer grapevine. If Topps prints 30 percent more cards than Fleer in a given season, then everyone knows the equivalent star card of the Fleer will be worth more than the Topps.

It's safe to say that there are at least a few billion cards printed every year, because Upper Deck admits to at least a 700-million mintage, or about a million cards per player.

Obviously, it doesn't pay to even try to guess. Certain companies enjoy a good reputation among dealers; others suffer bad ones. Topps, for instance, is known throughout the nation as the wholesaler's most responsive supplier. Its reputation among dealers is exceptionally good. It prints its cards early, and it prints them often, and it never creates an artificial demand for current cards. All it cares about—and it's all any honorable company should care about—is that it sells lots of cards at the manufactured price.

But Topps' image does fall short of saintly. It is not averse to reaping the rewards of any kind of publicity because, as everyone knows, publicity sells cards. In 1990, for instance, Topps printed a limited edition of 100 cards of President Bush posing during his playing days at Yale as a varsity ball player. Topps claims that all 100 cards were packaged and sent to Bush as a gift. Meanwhile, a Champaign, Illinois, card dealer discovered a Bush card in a wax pack. One of his customers is suing the dealer, claiming he offered it for sale at 15 cents. The matter will likely be settled in court. Later during the 1990 season, two other cards were "found."

My point is, how could this extremely rare Bush card accidentally find its way into general circulation? Wouldn't the firm take utmost care with such an important printing? According to *The Wall Street Journal,* Topps considers the Champaign card "stolen property" and wants it back to give to the nation's First Fan. It's fine that Topps has such righteous indignation about a single far-flung baseball card, but I think most collectors would feel a lot better if the White House reported that Bush received only 99 cards (or 97, or whatever the figure should have been).

Topps has been around since 1951, and it is the most widely known company. Hence, the four competitors have had to come up with schemes to attract attention to themselves and "create" the demand and make the market. The most common one has been inventing the perception of limited availability, and at one time or another, I've heard dealers complain about Donruss and Fleer. If one of those companies had a bad year in sales, it was simple strategy to ensure that the following year's issue would be unavailable to distributors, wholesalers, dealers, and retailers.

A child could figure out what happens next. The collecting public is sadly told—often by dealers who steadfastly complain that a certain company just won't ship—that a given issue is impossible to get. Then, of course, that same collecting public wants it more, especially if the price goes up. It's the same basic psychology that New York City nightclubs have used to promote exclusivity. Even when the club was empty, management would place a bouncer at the door and guard it with a velvet rope. The more people were asked—no, told—to wait in line, the more they were denied entry, the more all this petty behavior was reported in the gossip columns of the local papers, and the more people wanted to spend their money there.

In baseball cards, the best example of this is the Donruss 1984 set, which happens to list for more than double any of the other standard-issue sets of that year, despite the fact that Fleer and Topps also contain that season's hot rookie card, Don Mattingly.

Most card shops carry current trade literature, and, at least at the onset, you should buy one of every magazine and newspaper you see. Here is a sampling of the titles you'll likely encounter: *Baseball Card News, Baseball Cards, Baseball Card Price Guide, Current Card Prices, Sports Card Trader, Beckett's Baseball Card Monthly,* and *Sports Collectors Digest.* (See the appendix at the end of this book for suggested references.) Even the Topps company publishes its own quarterly magazine now, and as you might expect, the articles are often geared to promote its own products.

You will want to subscribe first to *Sports Collectors Digest* (or SCD, as it's known in the business) because it's the single publication that dealers and collectors rely on for business news and price information. Published weekly by Krause Publications, Inc. (700 E. State St., Iola, WI 54990), it is considered the bible of the business. A yearly subscription is $39.95, and there are various upgrades for speedy delivery. Neurotic collectors and anxious dealers pay $772.75 to get their copies via Federal Express, three or four days earlier than the bulk of the second-class newspaper subscribers. Obviously, the faster you get SCD the better, because you may get the jump on a fellow investor by spotting a bargain earlier. (The advertising deadline is three weeks prior to the cover date, so when word trickles out that something is priced well below market value, it is often sold long before you open your copy, anyway.) But it's not necessary to be the first one in your neighborhood to get SCD. Soon you'll find excellent buys and spot trends that don't always find their way into SCD's pages. The reason to read a trade paper is to learn the business language and to familiarize yourself with general market behavior.

By the time you've scoured several weeks' worth of SCDs, you'll notice a familiar mix in its 280–350 pages. The advertising to editorial ratio is approximately 90–10, but many articles are well researched, informative, and often worth clipping and saving. In fact, since SCD regularly publishes large auction results, it's probably a good idea to keep the last half-year's or year's worth of issues stacked in your basement for reference.

Remember, the nation's dealers religiously read SCD, and this is where the prime market is made. For example, you'll note which superstars commonly appear at shows to sign autographs, and more important, you'll find out what items they're signing and what items they're not. (I'll go into a lot more detail about that later.)

MR. MINT'S MAXIM: *Seventy to 80 percent, sometimes more, of the ads in SCD are pushing current cards and merchandise you should ignore. You can spot them easily. In one part, the merchant proclaims something is a "limited" edition, and in the next part, he is willing to take one-third off the price if you buy 10, half if you buy 100, and so on. This dealer likely has all 10,000 items and is desperately trying to unload them.*

The second most relied upon publication is *Beckett's Baseball Card Monthly* (4887 Alpha Rd., Ste. 200, Dallas, TX 75244). This glossy is consumer-oriented, and the articles are generally untimely because of a publishing schedule that has a three-month lead time. So when Dr. Jim Beckett is thinking of running a story in January, you won't get to read it until April or May. A month in the baseball card industry is like a month in a dog's life; the market is fickle and changes frequently. But Beckett is well read and well respected by longtime hobbyists, and also by the kids who drive the current card prices. The first page precocious eighth graders turn to is "Weather Report," where the magazine lists which cards are "hot" and which are "cold." New collectors, however, will find far more useful information in its excellent question-and-answer feature.

Beckett and SCD both publish price guides of baseball cards, as do many other newspapers and magazines. They are rough gauges of the *retail* market, and they're usually edited to include only those numbered cards which have greater than face value. (Any other card is referred to as a common, which is the opposite of a journeyman or a star.) In the coin trade, there's a "blue" book (the dealers' "buy" prices) and a "red" book (the dealers' "sell" prices). Everything in the baseball card trade is geared to a "red" book, or sell, mentality. When you own something, and you want to find out what it's worth, you'll have to do a little basic math, which I'll explain later.

Since each guide is a little different, expect plenty of disagreement on certain difficult cards and sets. Beckett's and SCD's price guides are most useful for their "pluses" and "minuses," or ascending or descending carats, which indicate whether an item has gone up or down in price.

Both Krause Publications and Beckett publish annual price guides in book form, and you should buy one or both every year.

MR. MINT'S MAXIM: *Go to bed with an annual price guide, and read it as if you were skimming the dictionary. Scan the prices of your favorite stars of yesteryear; familiarize yourself with the general market. Memorize the card company abbreviations and the other fairly universal ones: RC, for rookie card; FC, for first card; ROY, for Rookie of the Year card; SP for single-printed and DP for double-printed. (Basically, double-printed means that there are twice as many of a particular card floating around than one that is single-printed.)*

You should know there is a distinction between a "rookie" card and a company's "first" card. Being what it is, the business has had a very long tussle with semantics about this sort of thing, and it still has not conclusively decided the pure meaning of both. Traditionally, a first card means the first appearance of a player on cardboard by a given company. The Mickey Mantle cards help explain what I mean. Mantle's first card ever was issued in 1951, #253 by the Bowman company. But most people consider his "rookie" card to be the famous and far more desirable Topps #311, which was issued in 1952. Is the Topps Mantle rookie card a true rookie card? Technically not, as the purists will constantly remind you.

One other thing: Often a rookie or first card of a major player has nothing to do with when he actually played his first official major-league season, especially as defined by the generally accepted official standards. For one, in the past, the card companies didn't always print the cards of new players immediately. Reggie Jackson, for instance, had 25 homers with Oakland in 1968, but Topps didn't get around to putting him on a card until 1969.

Today, the reverse is often true, mainly because they begin

printing the new season's cards earlier than ever, almost as soon as the current season ends. And card companies know that a hot rookie can breed hysteria in the marketplace and, hence, high sales for their current cards. The card companies make their best predictions on the new crop of rookies, and they're no better at it than a team's general manager. This is why you will see cards of potential stars like Steve Avery of Atlanta, Juan Gonzalez of Texas, and Luis Sojo of Toronto on cards, even though they'd barely played in any games by 1990's All-Star break. Todd Van Poppel, the Oakland A's young pitching phenom, only played a few games in 1990 at the AA minor league level. But in 1991 Upper Deck already issued a "rookie" card, which was immediately retailing for $2.50. This is a perfect example of an overpriced penny stock which has yet to perform. Will he be the next Nolan Ryan? Who knows?

If the logic surrounding this seems somewhat incomprehensible, don't fret. You only need to make some sense of what is often nonsensical in this business in order to thrive.

DEVELOPING
A FIELD OF INTEREST

In my 12 years as a part-time and full-time professional, the mentality of the baseball hobbyist I've come to know spans the universe. At the highest end of the scale, and perhaps the most sophisticated, there is multimillionaire Barry Halper, the part owner of the New York Yankees, who is considered by many to have the finest collection of cards and memorabilia outside the Baseball Hall of Fame in Cooperstown. Halper, a paper company owner from Newark, has every card ever made and the uniform of every Hall of Famer except Eppa Rixey and Ralph Kiner. Then there's a young kid who spends thousands of dollars with me on cards every year who won't even fix the frame on his eyeglasses. In between, there's a multitude of personalities, and I've learned never to be surprised.

Collectors are not abnormal people, but then again, they're not normal either. The more obsessive they are, the flakier they're likely to become. (I know because I collect Art Deco Verlys glass. When it comes to driving 600 miles to find an obscure piece, my behavior is as irrational as any other collector.) One new collector said to me that he's spending so

much money and time on baseball memorabilia that he wondered if there was a Betty Ford Center for this type of addiction.
He was sure he was headed there. One collector reneged on
selling me his lifelong collection. He told me he couldn't bear to
give it up. When I left his house, he was nearly in tears. (The
following year, however, amid a divorce, I eventually bought it.)

There are several levels of intensity, of course, and I recommend first that you don't dive in so deeply that baseball is
ruling your life. After a while you will probably fall comfortably
into a given mold, and I'm going to describe some of them for
you. Please disregard any tinge of underlying cynicism, because my labels are meant to illustrate what *kind* of people get
involved in the hobby. None are necessarily "bad" at what
they're doing; in fact, many do very well. Eventually you'll
become or meet types like these.

The Dabbler. This is a guy who just collects haphazardly.
There's no philosophy to what he's stuffing in his display
cabinets or hanging on the den walls. There's a Mets pennant
from 1969 here, and an autographed 1980 Phillies team ball
there, and an incomplete set of 1963 Topps cards in varying
condition. There is nothing wrong with dabbling, but understand that if you fall into this niche, you're probably never
going to assemble a meaningful collection that accumulates
equity. You'll enjoy what you have, and some of your items may
have good investment potential. But as a whole, you'll have a
portfolio so spotty and scattered that it will never be worth as
much as you hope.

The Accumulator. The personality who buys more than one
piece of a given item of memorabilia is often a puzzling one. He
has to have a lot of something, often good items, but one is
never enough. It's a dozen identical Hank Aaron cards and five
identical Stan Musials, and then there are three sets of 1975
Topps cards (but no other year), five Mickey Mantle autographed balls, and so on. No matter how many Pee Wee Reeses
he had, he's the guy who wouldn't trade one back in grade

school. The Accumulator is a serious Dabbler. He'll double his equity in some of his low-priced investments, but it will take a long time, and then he probably won't sell. Accumulators love to boast about how many of some esoteric item they own. If I offered 100 percent of the book value for all but one of those Aarons, he'd say no thanks. He might sell one, though.

The Hoarder. The Hoarder is one of those classic personalities who have to shovel as much stuff through their garage door as they possibly can. He has 100 sets of 1989 Fleers, just because he got a fantastic deal from a wholesaler who couldn't wait to dump them. It doesn't matter whether the price of the set increases or decreases to the Hoarder, because *he's* holding them. Maybe forever. When he claims he doubled his money on cards, and you ask how long it took, he needs a calculator to count the years. When someone mentions a hot card, like the 1989 Ken Griffey, Jr., rookie card, he says, "Oh, I've got a hundred of them."

The Speculator. This is your typical, impressionable nouvelle hobbyist who buys only what's seemingly fashionable, usually current cards or collectibles. Like the Hoarder, the Speculator buys large lots of certain items, but the Speculator is looking to make a fast profit, so he's always on the lookout to sell. If he buys 100 sets of cards at $23, and then sells them for $25, he's made $200. It usually takes longer than he thinks. Like six months or more. Occasionally, he hits a big score. He is not much different from the guy who calls his broker and buys a stock because his brother-in-law just bought it.

The True Collector. Since "collector" is such a catchall description, I'd like to distinguish the True Collector from all the pretenders. He's the quiet, inwardly emotional guy who slowly, methodically, and meticulously assembles a body of arcane items in a single category. He has a specialty, like the 1969 Mets or the 1961 Yankees or All-Star game autographed baseballs. He considers himself an expert in his specialty, and he very well is, but he's humble enough not to make a point of it. He's a buyer, not a seller, unless he's upgrading an item. Most important, he's satisfied to have one great specimen of something he desires. He'll spend a lot of time, effort, and money to search out what he wants, and he'll doggedly pursue the impossible, especially if it means completing a phase of his collection.

The Impatient Investor. He's usually wearing a three-piece suit, and he's an innocuous middle-aged man from Anywhere, America. He doesn't know a lot about cards and doesn't really make his own trades. He'll never know the difference between a Cal Hubbard and a Carl Hubbell, and he doesn't care. He trusts a dealer to assemble his portfolio, and as long as he feels like he's not being taken, he'll continue to keep sending the dealer checks. He wants to sell as fast as he buys. He likes action, even though he has no idea what he owns at any given moment.

The Prudent Investor. He's a guy often found in a suit, too, but he might also be a slick teenager with a surf T-shirt roaming a card show, hustling sets of cards. He knows that to do well, he must invest his time, proceed carefully but swiftly, and he understands that not everything he touches will yield windfall profits. He is knowledgeable and has foresight. Most of all, he'll part with an item as soon as he feels he's received a fair return on his investment. What the Prudent Investors have in common is this: the desire to make a few serious moves, take modest profits, and make few mistakes. These guys have high batting averages.

Of the seven types of general profiles I've offered, which one do you suspect you'll become? It's a trick question, of course. At one time or another, you'll likely drift into and out of more than one category or create your own. In order to make money without losing your hair, my advice is to develop into some kind of cross between the True Collector and the Prudent Investor. And then, like it or not, you're a casual dealer.

When I made the transition from collector to dealer, I sold my entire collection en masse, accumulating some $40,000 to $50,000. It cost less to put together, sure, but I don't even remember how much profit I made. Why? Profit wasn't the motive then. I didn't care. What I had was a collection, built over a period of time, and not a bunch of commodities that I was buying and selling immediately. Now I do it full-time, day and night, 40 weekends a year, and I operate my business with employees, office rent, advertising, and other kinds of overhead. You don't. One important difference between a collector/investor and a dealer is the length of time you own the object. The faster you sell something, the closer you are to becoming a dealer.

MR. MINT'S MAXIM: *In order to gain a return on your investment, you must sell what you bought. A "paper" profit is just that. Whether you're a True Collector or a Prudent Investor, never fall in love with anything you've bought. Be prepared to disown it for the right price at any time.*

Buyer's remorse is a syndrome everyone experiences at one time or another—Do I really like it that much? Did I overpay?—but excessive seller's sentiment will give you nightmares and leave you broke. Acquire a resolve that everything you own is for sale at the right price.

If I spot an item I think I can sell, I buy it regardless of whether I like it. But the more I like something, the more enthusiasm it generates in the old collector in me, and the more I'm willing to pay. Subsequently, I know it will be easier to resell it, even if I make only a small profit.

Once you've had a taste of card collecting, you'll want to

move on. Trust me. Cards are just the first stage of addiction. There's a common belief among many dealers and new collectors that it's "too late" to put money into cards. That's not true at all, especially if you're buying the right ones. What these folks really mean is that there are wider opportunities in the memorabilia aspect of the business. I'm very bullish on true antiques and noncard collectibles of any kind in baseball, because there are few price guides. Baseball memorabilia is just like any other antique, any other collectible. When you spot that lovely Early American sideboard at a flea market— one you've never seen in all your years of browsing—how do you know what it's worth? Truly? You don't. It's what you're willing to pay and what the owner is willing to take.

The best baseball items—signed, "game-used," bats, balls, gloves, hats—are getting more difficult to find and usually are fairly expensive compared with cards. If you've got a decent-sized budget, you might want to jump first into collectibles. I know one new collector who didn't want to waste any time with cards, because he couldn't display them. He buys signed bats and balls, and he concentrates on the 1950s Brooklyn Dodgers and 1960s New York Yankees.

MR. MINT'S MAXIM: *Think quality, not quantity. It is a better investment to buy a few truly great objects than several good, mediocre, or marginal ones.*

I cannot emphasize enough the need to specialize, if for no other reason than for the educational value. By honing in on a narrow phase of collecting, even if you eventually abandon it, you will quickly learn how the business works and become an expert in the market quirks of that particular specialty. The guy with the greatest Satchel Paige cache probably knows as much about the subtle fluctuations in the Paige market as most dealers.

A few years ago, Steve Reeves, a part-time dealer from Rockville, Maryland, began collecting and investing in "Exhibits," or cards from the Exhibit Supply Company manufactured in the 1920s. These large, 3⅜" by 5⅜" black and white cards were originally sold for pennies in arcade machines. Exhibit made not only baseball cards but wrestling, boxing, and movie star cards. Reeves began putting classified ads in SCD saying he was a buyer. He just had an instinct. They were attractive, in nice condition, inexpensive except for a few big-name cards, and most of all, very available. Part-time flea marketers who couldn't sell many on weekends sent Reeves their Exhibits by the boxful. Now the market is beginning to rise steadily—collectors are always looking for the "next hot thing"—and everyone who is buying or selling makes his first call to Reeves, now known as the Exhibit Man. While he hasn't cornered the market, he's created a very nice niche for himself.

I relate this story not to encourage you to become a dealer, or necessarily to plunk a few thousand into Exhibits. Reeves asked himself the questions, What area of the business hasn't yet been saturated? Where's a potential opportunity for realistic, long-term market growth? For years, dealers at shows teased Reeves about his Exhibits, and now they're a legitimate collectible.

As you get more comfortable, you must focus on a single, specific area of baseball nostalgia. Try putting together a complete set of cards from a famous team. Or perhaps you'll want the definitive collection on Hall of Famers elected between 1960 and 1980. Let your imagination simmer. Here are a few ideas to ponder before you create your own:

- ◆ World Series or All-Star game programs and scorecards
- ◆ Autographed 8" by 10" glossy news photos of a famous team or Hall of Fame players
- ◆ Ticket stubs from famous games or ballparks
- ◆ Player contracts or autographed letters

- ◆ Stadium seats from the grand old parks
- ◆ Single-signed baseballs of Hall of Famers
- ◆ Team-signed baseballs of famous teams
- ◆ Press pins from All-Star games or the World Series
- ◆ Anything you can find from the 1960 Pittsburgh Pirates, or any other "special" team in baseball history
- ◆ Anything you can find about Jackie Robinson, or any other Hall of Fame player you grew up watching
- ◆ Negro-leagues memorabilia, especially posters and score-cards
- ◆ Memorabilia from members of the 500 Home Run Club or the 3,000 Strike Out Club or the 300 Win Club
- ◆ Memorabilia from pitchers who pitched no-hitters or perfect games
- ◆ Most Valuable Players, Cy Young Award winners, or Rookies of the Year of, say, a given period, league, or decade
- ◆ Memorabilia from a famous game, such as the 1933 All-Star game or Don Larsen's perfect World Series game

Some collectors develop a specialty by random intervention. One real estate magnate in New York, who is a lifelong baseball fan, received a ball autographed by Ty Cobb and Babe Ruth as a 50th birthday gift from his son. He was astonished that it cost $2,250. But it rekindled his passion for the heroes of the game, and he has set a goal to get a signature on a ball of every player, manager, and official inducted into the Hall of Fame. That gift cost him a lot of money, because he now has roughly three-fourths of the single-signed balls of the 208 baseball men enshrined at Cooperstown.

MR. MINT'S MAXIM: *Just collecting autographs on any item that floats your way is not a narrow enough field of interest to constitute a valuable collection. If*

*your signatures are on postcards, checks, glossies,
and scorecards, when it comes time to sell, dealers
will look askance at many of the items. It's easier for
them to place a premium on a legitimate, carefully
compiled collection than a lot of odds and ends.*

If you decide to acquire, for example, a signed publicity
photograph by every member of the 1961 Yankees (a difficult
but not impossible task), then you have zeroed in on a
specialty.

When you finally choose the area that you're going to begin
mining for gems, remember to strike a healthy balance between
the stuff that everyone seems to collect and the stuff that
nobody cares about. For example, I wouldn't suggest becoming
enamored with 1977 Pepsi Glove Discs, a 72-player set of
promotional tabs that came in soda cans. (There was an
emphasis on Cleveland Indians and Cincinnati Reds players,
probably because Pepsi was test-marketing in those two cities.)
It's a cheap set, maybe $15 to $20, and you won't find it on
dealers' tables at shows, but that's not why it's not a worthwhile
investment. It's a bad idea because those kinds of esoteric
items do not have many buyers. On the other hand, a complete
set of 180 1962 plastic coins found in Salada tea and Junket
pudding mixes is something with much larger collector demand. The book value of the "Saladas," as they're known, is well
into many thousands of dollars, even though some individual
coins still cost only a few dollars.

All this means is that in any marketplace driven by the classic
law of supply and demand, one factor will overwhelm the other
in terms of a price rise or decline. In baseball cards, demand is
often more important than supply.

The supply of baseball cards and memorabilia is driven by
two characteristics: scarcity and rarity. At first, you might
wonder what the difference between the two is, but I draw an
important distinction. Scarcity refers to an item's actual mint-

age, or how many were made in the first place. Rarity relates more to how many of what was made actually survived, and how many of those items actually surface on the market.

Demand is simple. How many collectors want the item?

Let's see how rarity, scarcity, and demand blend together to produce a truly valuable piece. Take the 1911 Philadelphia Athletics Shibe Park press pin, the first pin ever issued (though the first World Series game was played in 1903). In 1911, television was a dream, there were no radio journalists, only newspaper reporters and perhaps a few magazine writers specializing in baseball. How many reporters could have covered that Series? How many of those pins were actually manufactured? Let's say 15 or 20, even 30 on the high end. How many actually survived with the ribbon intact? Maybe five, 10 if you're a true optimist. That is the reason why they trade in the $15,000 to $20,000 range. Few are around, and many serious high-end collectors covet them. Once somebody finds one, he's not wont to part with it.

Let's take another example with two baseball cards. The first is the coveted Honus Wagner T-206 tobacco card issued by Piedmont in 1909–11. The Wagner is commonly (though erroneously) referred to by the popular press as the "rarest" card ever made. There are likely to be somewhere between 20 and 30 Wagner cards in existence—I've bought and sold seven different ones. A great specimen is easily worth more than $115,000, and privately, I've heard that someone refused $300,000 for his Wagner. The T-206 series was the most popular issue of its time, and Wagner is inarguably in the top dozen of the most famous players of all time. The tiny card itself is magical, the Mona Lisa of the business. There's Wagner's beautiful, rosy cheeks under soulful eyes, framed by a boyish face. There is myth behind the card, and two stories have been told about why there are so few. First, Wagner didn't approve of tobacco, so he enjoined Piedmont from printing his picture on the cards, but only after a few came off the press. The second one, favored by cynics, is that Wagner had a dispute with Piedmont, who wouldn't meet his endorsement fee demand.

Which story you believe is immaterial. The point is that it's the single most desired baseball card. It is not the rarest. The rarest is probably the Fred Lindstrom card in the 1932 U.S. Caramel Card set. Only one card is known to exist. In that set U.S. Caramel produced 32 cards of baseball stars, including a few standouts in other sports, like golf and boxing. They made one card, the Lindstrom, in an extremely limited quantity. The reason was that anyone who found the Lindstrom could redeem it for a new bicycle. Now, Lindstrom was a Hall of Fame player, but he was no Ruth or Gehrig. The Ruths and Gehrigs were made in larger quantities by Caramel, because the company was selling candy and not cards. They wanted their customers to collect the popular players (which was also the equivalent of collecting the advertising—may we remind you to buy our candy while you're admiring the cards?). Why they chose Lindstrom for the prize is anyone's guess. But how many people do you think didn't redeem the card for a bicycle? Well, the dealer who bought the one known card paid $25,000 for it, and he's been offered only $15,000. It may be the rarest card in the world, even "the toughest," but then again the demand is not there.

MR. MINT'S MAXIM: *Until you're absolutely comfortable, do not venture into objects that do not have a "book" value in a price guide.*

While I've never made a mistake on the level of the Lindstrom buy, I frequently make lesser errors in judgment when I see an item I've never seen before. I like it, I offer what I think is a fair price, but then I can't sell it, because I can't find a buyer. If you haven't seen something before, and you're still a relative novice, then resist the urge to make an immediate offer without researching the demand.

LEARNING TO GRADE CARDS
(and Other Object Lessons About Condition)

Several years ago, a collector approached my table at a card show with a complete set of 1953 Topps baseball cards. It was the most beautiful set of 1953s I'd ever seen in my experience as a dealer and collector. The cards were still glossy, the edges were crisp; they looked as if they'd just been pulled off the printing press. Since you just don't see great cards like this every day, I was quite the excited dealer. So I took out a ruler and measured one. It was 2⅝ by 3¾ inches, the manufactured size. Then I quickly checked the Mantle, Robinson, Mays, and Satchel Paige cards—the four standouts, and the most expensive cards in the set—and they were in perfect shape. Since I've handled millions of cards in my day, I hastily shuffled through the the remaining 269 cards to make sure they were all there and there were no weird printing deficiencies. They were terrific.

I offered the seller $1,700, which was book value at the time. He wanted $2,100, and then I offered $1,900. He accepted the deal without hesitation. Ten percent over book for cards like this was still an excellent buy.

I took the set over to a friend's table, another dealer named

John Broggi, and showed him the cards. Broggi, of course, knew a buyer for gems like these, and he immediately gave me $2,400 for the set.

About three hours later, Broggi returned to my table with a long, grave look, to put it conservatively. He was carrying the coveted 1953 Topps set under his arm.

"Um, Alan, I hate to tell you this," he said, "but did you look at the backs of these cards?"

Well, I hadn't, but I did then. On the back of every single card was "LG." Whoever had owned them was so proud and possessive he had rubber-stamped his initials in the upper left-hand corner where the official number was printed in the baseball circle.

The cards were essentially worthless, devalued by a stupid mistake. Any card that's altered or adulterated in any way is worth less than it was in its original condition. (Autographed cards, by the way, lower the card's value, because 90 percent of the collecting public want their autographs on something other than a baseball card. Call it eccentric, but nobody said people in this business weren't eccentric.)

But I'm telling you this story for another reason. I made a bigger mistake than LG, because I bought the cards without looking at a single reverse side. Had I checked one card, I would have politely told LG, or whoever was selling the set, that there was little interest in cards with someone's initials on them. The great Mr. Mint was humbled, not to mention the hit I took for $1,900 because I gave Broggi's money back to him.

In order to succeed in the baseball collectibles marketplace, you must learn how to grade both cards and memorabilia. Even if you don't plan on straying into the other territory (cards versus various memorabilia), it's a good idea to understand the difference between an ordinary, worn 50-year-old baseball and an exquisite, mint example. But remember, grading cards is more difficult and important than grading anything else in the business. Understanding the different characteristics of cards is perhaps more exacting and filled with minutiae than with grading other baseball objets d'art. You cannot hope to master this overnight. You must inspect a lot of cards, new and old, and discuss them with dealers and other collectors until you're absolutely adept at describing and rating them.

MR. MINT'S MAXIM: *If you've ever been involved in real estate, you've heard the broker explain the three most important aspects of a given property's worth: location, location, and location. In baseball cards, I have a similar saying: condition, condition, and condition. Off-grade cards do not increase in value at the same rate as top-quality cards. Similarly, off-grade material does not sell as well or as quickly as the top-graded items. In a deep recession they may not sell at all. If you expect to resell a card or object, do not buy anything (except extremely rare items) unless it is in near mint or mint condition.*

One of the simple psychological techniques shrewd real estate salesmen use when they attempt to sell houses is to always begin showing the lower-quality ones first, regardless of the buyer's price range. They may schedule a trip to three homes, $200,000, $250,000, then $300,000, even if they know the high end of your budget is $250,000. Before they slam the car door shut, they know the only one you'll remotely be interested in is the one costing $300,000. Calling salesmen like this shrewd isn't meant in any way to be derogatory. They are manipulating buyers, of course, but they are also priming or educating them about the higher premium placed on quality goods.

The same thing is true with the baseball card salesman. At one card show in the summer of 1990, I saw a collector checking a table for 1980 Topps Rickey Henderson rookie cards. Henderson was closing in on Lou Brock's all-time stolen-base record, and this card had been rising in price steadily, despite the fact that they were plentiful. The dealer had displayed none, and when the collector inquired about them, he replied that he had several in varying condition. Could he see them? Of course. He pulled out three, all individually stored in plastic holders. They were all $75 each, and on close inspection they were slightly worn. The collector asked if he had anything nicer. Of course. The next three were all perfect cards, each in individual screw-down Lucite holders, and they were priced at $125. The collector bought one of the nicer ones, despite the dealer's unwillingness to part with one for $100. Did the collector make a good buy? Certainly. Even though book value was $100 (he paid $25 more), by the end of the 1990 season, Henderson's card was booking in the $200 to $250 range. The price of Rickey's card doubled in six months despite the fact that he was two bases shy of breaking the record.

MR. MINT'S MAXIM: *If you buy the highest-quality card you can find, then when you're ready to sell it, you only have one thing to argue about: price.*

By now, you should have read both Beckett's and SCD's little summaries of grading, ranging from poor, fair, good, very good, excellent, near mint, and mint. If life in this business were simple, the baseball gods would automatically confer one of those seven designations on every card ever minted. But it's not. Grading a card is a subjective thing, and over the years the seven categories have stretched into a dozen or more. In advertisements, you'll see cryptic abbreviations that say NR MT + + or VG-EX + or some such combination of hieroglyphic that illustrates all kinds of hedging on the part of the seller. The more elusive and elliptical the description is, the more wary you should be.

As an exercise for this book, I investigated the price differentiation among the Reggie Jackson rookie card during a one-week period in 1990.

Here is the first group of conditions and selling prices I gleaned from the June 1 and June 8, 1990, issues of SCD. (By the way, the SCD Weekly Price Guide listed the card in the June 1 issue at $450 in NR MT and $180 in EX. Note that one formal grade in condition here is equal to 2½ times the price of the lower grade.)

REGGIE JACKSON ROOKIE CARD,
1969 Topps #260

NR MT/MT	$495
MT	$760
EX	$150
NM + 35–65	$595
NR MT− o/c [off center]	$150
NM+	$800
NR MT + o/c [off center]	$300
VG+	$170
NM/MT	$525
NM 70–30	$385
EX/MT	$315
EX+	$260
EX	$180
Poor (very ugly)	$28
VG/EX	$188
Corner wear that can be seen w/o magnifying glass, well centered, no creases	$260
NR MT/MT 40–60	$760

NM+ 50–50	$450
NM/MT	$575
NR MT	$295

The following prices on the same Jax card were recorded at a large baseball card show on Long Island on June 8, 1990. The prices in parentheses were reductions immediately offered by the dealer as soon as I asked to look at them:

EX MT+	$425
VG	$225
EX	$250
NR MT	$450
NR MT 20–80	$400
NR MT/MT	$600
NR MT/MT	$750
EX (bent corner)	$195
EX/NR MT (cockeyed)	$475
NR MT/MT (slightly crooked)	$525 ($450)
NR MT 20–80 top-bottom	$325
EX	$300 ($250)
VG	$200
VG	$200
VG/EX	$275 ($125)

The above prices will undoubtedly be outdated by the time this book is published, but that is not what matters. The table I've compiled is important because it gives a wide sense of asking price as well as condition among 35 different specimens of the same card. The selling prices are merely reference points to illustrate how convoluted and subjective grading is among dealers. The references to "cockeyed" and "slightly crooked" refer to the centering of the portrait in relation to the borders. I'll explain more about this later in the chapter. One "very good" card is $225 and another graded "excellent" is $250.

Why is there that small a disparity in price over an entire grade? Because somebody (probably several dealers, actually) doesn't know how to grade or is intentionally misgrading the card.

Look how many intermediate-condition cards are available for $200 to $375. The highest prices include 13 cards at $450 (the price guide quote) and up, or about a third of what's offered. Four cards are more than $600. Since it's impossible to inspect every card, it's difficult to tell which card was an excellent buy. Only one dealer called his card pure mint, and it was $760. There was nothing at all wrong with the card, of course, but it was higher priced than equivalent cards I'd seen in flawless condition.

After studying this table—and realizing that these were all asking prices—a serious buyer should have been able to procure a near mint card or better for somewhere between $400 and $500 in that market.

Since I'm only recommending you buy the two highest-grade cards, mint and near mint, I'm not going to waste space here describing the various characteristics of the off-grades, except when they relate to an otherwise near perfect card. To me, anything below the near mint designation must contain the word "excellent" in it, and excellent means the card is worn.

Most experienced, professional card dealers and collectors do not know how to properly grade a card, because they often confuse the difference between *condition* and *characteristic.*

Condition refers strictly to wear.

Characteristics refer to the quality of the printing on a particular card.

The proper way to grade is to first describe the condition and then the printing characteristics. When it comes to the formal description, the two are wholly unrelated. (But when it comes to financial appraisal, of course, they are closely related.)

What is the definition of "mint"? Simply stated, "new as

manufactured." It doesn't necessarily mean perfect. Let's say that you bought a dozen unopened wax packs of 1985 Topps cards, and you opened them up and found three Roger Clemens cards. Since you handled them first yourself, you already know they are absolutely and truly "from the mint," as long as you don't screw one up while you're inspecting them.

Now, one of the Clemens cards has a tiny red ink dot on his jersey, and another is off center 70–30, left to right. You did not cause these minor defects; the Topps manufacturing process did. These defects are the characteristics of the cards. Upon close inspection, you find no distinguishing characteristics on the third card. It is perfectly centered, 50–50, top and bottom, left to right. The printing on the reverse is perfect. Though they are all in mint condition, only the third one will bring the top market price.

Just because a card is mint doesn't mean it doesn't have defects. Card companies did not produce baseball cards to be perfect. They printed them only as a marketing venture to sell gum or tobacco. I've seen 30-year-old cards that were never handled until I opened the pack, only to discover they were totally ruined by tiny bugs who bore small holes through them in their quest to get at the sugar in the bubble gum. They were mint, but they were now damaged and worthless.

When learning how to grade, develop a habit of looking at a card the same way every time. When someone describes an expensive card to me on the telephone, I begin drawing a picture in my mind of exactly what I think it looks like.

My particular method is to start at the top left-hand corner, then the bottom, then the top right, then the bottom right. Why start with corners? These are spots that get the most wear, the first nicks, and it's usually where the cardboard begins to separate. Then I check the overall characteristics, like centering, gloss, the cut, and the reverse. In order to check the gloss, or a card's "shine," you must reflect the face of the card in bright light. If there are any surface defects or light gum stains, sometimes this is the only way they'll appear. At many card shows, the lighting is abysmally low. If that's the case, ask to inspect any card you're interested in under a lamp.

MR. MINT'S MAXIM: *When you're inspecting a card in a screw-down Lucite holder, it is imperative that you ask the seller to unscrew it and remove the card. Faint creases on the card's surface are masked by the holder and are seldom noticeable under plastic. Plastic is fine, but it's often difficult to tell whether the card is creased or the plastic is scratched.*

In the past two years, a card's centering—how well the portrait fits on the card, or how even the bordering is—has become a critical characteristic in determining its ultimate value.

In one auction I held, I had a 1952 Topps Mickey Mantle card that came from my famous "find." The card was absolutely gem mint, the colors were bright, the corners were razor-sharp, and the borders were white as snow. But the card had to be classified as "off center," meaning about 70–30. This card is probably the most expensive postwar card on the market. But instead of bringing somewhere around $15,000 for the card, I advised the consignor to put a reserve bid on it of about $7,500. The Topps printing press cost this guy about $7,500, but that's the way the cards are cut.

MR. MINT'S MAXIM: *The acceptable cutoff point for centering is 60–40. In short, anything worse is not a worthwhile investment. When using the catchall* *phrase "well centered," most honest, reliable dealers mean 60–40 or 55–45. But you must understand their reasoning to even include the description. "Well centered" does not mean perfectly centered, or 50–50; otherwise, it would be so stated.*

What do "near mint" and "near mint to mint" actually mean? The first designation means the card is nearly perfect, but under a very close look you'll spot a single minor flaw, often one soft corner. The second designation was coined merely to split hairs. Sometimes it describes a range of cards in the set (that is, some are near mint, others are mint), and sometimes it means the tiniest of flaws in an otherwise perfect card.

It should be obvious even to a novice collector that it's far more difficult to find the highest quality in cards that are very old. Although SCD carefully reminds its readers each week what its tables in the price guides actually mean, be aware that cards listed from 1980 to the present have two columns, mint and near mint (MT, NR MT). The cards listed prior to 1981 are listed in two columns, near mint and excellent (NR MT, EX). So, if you're following me so far, this means that you should be ignoring pre-1980 cards that grade in the right-hand, or EX, column.

There has been a recent movement in the business to professionally grade baseball cards. Two different enterprises, Superlative Baseball Card Certification and Acu-Card, have been spreading the idea that it is preferable to assign a numerical value or rating to a given card. At best, this is an attempt at the impossible, which is to transform something that is totally subjective into something coldly objective. At worst, it's a detriment to the hobby and the business, an absolutely horrific idea. The theory is that for a fee ranging from $27 to $110 per card (depending on the speed of service), three "independent and objective card experts" (a direct quote from one of Superlative's ads) will examine and ascertain the "exact quality" of a card.

Here is the comparison that Superlative gives for its grades along with the accepted equivalent nomenclature in the business:

10	poor
20	fair
30	good
40	very good
50	very good/excellent
55–65	excellent
70–75	excellent/near mint
80	near mint
84–88	near mint/mint
92–96	mint
98–100	gem mint

When I was at a large convention in Long Beach, California, in February 1989, I asked one of the founders of this grading system to rate the 1955 Sandy Koufax card that I had. He said it was a 92. I was angry and perplexed. How could I have a card that was only a 92 if I took it out of the pack myself and didn't hurt it? Well, he took a few points off because he didn't like the back of the card. He took another few points off because it was not perfectly white. No card is 100, he said. Not even the brand-new 1991 cards that every kid in the country is opening? No. (Incidentally, the Superlative ratings above do not say where a 53 or an 82 fits in the contemporary scheme of grading. I suppose a 53 means "very good/excellent to excellent" and an 82 means "near mint to near mint/mint." Are you thoroughly confused? You should be. There are two things a grader wants you to believe. One, that an 82 is one point better than an 81. And two, that only a grading service is qualified to rate a card and that you cannot be.)

To me, and to most experienced dealers, this logic is ludicrous. The professional graders are trying to turn the art into an exact science. And this will do nothing but cause ill will in the future.

The people who profess to grade cards are simply taking advantage of a public that is already fickle about condition, by putting it onto a level where ordinary collectors cannot have access to understanding it.

The most cogent argument that the grading companies can make in order to justify their existence is that numerical grading will attract new people into the business with more money to invest. It can only attract very wealthy people who have no time to spend learning about any kind of investment instrument. These people will expect an unreasonably high return on their dollar, and when they don't reap it, they will be angry. Nobody likes to see a bull market and high prices more than I do in this business, but when I was asked to become a charter member of Superlative, I refused, despite the fact I could have received large revenues.

MR. MINT'S MAXIM: *Numerical grading of baseball cards will* artificially *and unfairly (to both buyer and seller) inflate the prices of top-quality cards. If you buy a numerically graded card, you'll pay for the grading, and chances are you'll overpay for the card.*

A few additional points about numerical grading. The actual cost of the grading, even at $27, is prohibitive for the $100 card, which is the cornerstone of the midlevel investor. Why would anyone want to spend 27 percent of a card's perceived value to get it professionally graded? This type of treatment can only insult the surviving quality of any very old, valuable cards. If a dealer gets a $4,000 Ty Cobb card graded and it's only a 70, the novice buyer still has no idea whether it's the best Cobb he'll ever find or whether there are a couple of dozen more for sale with an 80 or better. So the dealer then informs the potential buyer that he's not likely to find a better one. And the collector, who is new and cautious, feels (rightfully) that he's being hyped. It's a no-win situation.

Robert Schmierer, the promoter of the respected Willow Grove, Pennsylvania, show (which has been running since 1975, longer than the National Convention, by the way), has refused to rent table space to the card grading companies. Schmierer points out that the confusion that numerical grading will add to an already complicated part of the business could cause its demise. I agree. But if I'm wrong and this idea catches on, then I'll be either forced to go along with such a system or become a day laborer instead of a baseball card dealer. (As this book went to press, the card grading services were experiencing financial difficulties. It looks as though the idea will not catch on, although there is a very respected coin dealer who is still trying to muster support for a system much less complicated than Superlative's.)

What if somebody decides there should be numerical criteria assigned to describing the condition of a bat or a pennant or a ball? Already, dealers are describing autographed baseballs on a scale of 1 to 10 (from worst to best).

World Series programs, uniforms, board games, ticket stubs, bats, balls, spikes, batting gloves, pennants, and press pins and the like are not viewed with the same microscopic intensity as baseball cards. Nevertheless, condition plays a crucial role in price, so you should be aware of what's investment quality and what isn't.

In general, when you see midrange descriptions (good, very good, excellent) of old programs, board games, and other paper-goods pieces of memorabilia, you can expect to notice a good deal of wear. The spine of an old magazine will be worn, the paper will be yellowed somewhat or considerably, the corners may be bent or contain slight tears. An ancient baseball board game should contain all the pieces, but expect it to be well handled and in used condition. Nobody bought those things 30 or 40 years ago with the intention of putting them in the closet without opening or playing them. Look for wear on the box, which is usually torn or broken in one of the four corners. Unless these items in off condition are extremely rare, my advice is to pass on them. The naive collector who just bought a fairly worn copy of the first issue of *Sports Illustrated* is usually astonished to discover how common that issue is, especially in mint condition. Every sports fan seemed to save it, and there are always three or four for sale at every card show.

MR. MINT'S MAXIM: *The theory of buying only the top condition is the same for baseball memorabilia, yet thankfully, grading these items is a lot less complicated than grading cards. Consequently, there are fewer disputes.*

Bats have enjoyed an increasing amount of popularity in the past few years, and scrutinizing their condition is relatively uncomplicated. A bat is either "new," "game-used" (scuffed), "cracked," or "repaired." Very old, used bats made personally for the stars with their autographs are the most valuable. The least valuable ones are new, unused bats with factory inscriptions of the player's name, but not made exclusively for the player's use. These are called *store* bats because they're sold by sporting goods retailers, and they usually take on a collectible value only when a player signs one. (Bats themselves are quite complex due to the different levels of manufacturing, however. I don't recommend you buy any bats until you read the chapter on memorabilia and thoroughly study the market.)

Autographed balls may be the second most collected item after cards, so their condition does require some extended explanation. Baseballs are frequently described with the same designations as cards; that is, poor, fair, good, excellent, near mint, and mint. Today, with all the attention to the current star autographed market, most balls are official National or American League balls and are in mint condition. They can be purchased through ads in SCD or at local sporting goods stores. Years ago, however, before the hobby became a business, fans collected signatures on baseballs and tossed them in a drawer in the family room. The kids might have had a catch with a Mel Ott or Hank Greenberg ball. Or they left them on a windowsill. The object might have been coveted, but care for it was unsophisticated. Therefore, many of the great signed baseballs from the 1930s and earlier haven't survived in terrific condition. The horsehide has worn or been scuffed, the whiteness of the ball has been faded by sunlight. The fountain or quill pen signature has lightened or, worse, smudged. Very old near mint and mint balls do exist, of course, but they're difficult to find and naturally bring premium prices.

Luckily, serious and responsible dealers have been describing autographed balls in ads in much more detail than they do cards. If a ball is called only "very good," usually it will say why.

Most owners of a single old ball have no idea about its condition. At one show, a woman approached me with a Babe Ruth autographed ball. It had yellowed slightly, and some of the horsehide had cracked, especially near the signature. Now the signature was dark, very bold, and beautiful; in fact, I told her I'd seen fewer nicer Ruth autographs. She had heard that single-signed Babe Ruth balls brought $5,000. Yes, near mint balls, in cream or off-white as they were made in that era. Hers was worth perhaps $2,000 to $2,500 at the most, because the ball was only in good to very good condition. The very nicest Ruth ball I'd seen had sold for $7,500. So that gives you an idea of the range—at least $5,000—of a Babe Ruth ball based solely on condition.

BASEBALL ARCHAEOLOGY: WHERE TO FIND GREAT BUYS

The art of buying baseball cards and other collectibles was relatively easy to master when I first started in the 1970s. The fraternity of collectors was much smaller, intimate, and informal. There were no dealers around using phrases like "investment grade" or "sports card commodities" in their advertising and promotional literature. Finding excellent pieces, real artifacts of baseball lore, was more of a scavenger hunt, and frequently I found myself leafing through old shoe boxes in some strange living room in a town I'd never dreamed existed.

Collections still creep out of the woodwork of old homes, but finds are fewer than ever. One reason for this is that some folks have the stuff and don't want it to be found; they don't need the money. There are still collections waiting to be discovered, but the trail is a long, arduous, speculative one. In the past, word of mouth was enough. You were visiting a relative in a Chicago suburb, and someone at a cocktail party mentioned the grandson of a guy who worked for a local distributor or the trucking company who had a candy store route. Oh? And he saved boxes of cards. And he never opened them? you asked innocently.

One of my greatest discoveries was when I found some 5,500 cards from the 1954 and 1955 Topps series in their original wax packs. A retired wholesaler who lived in Paris, Tennessee, had left them in a beat-up old station wagon parked in the back of his driveway.

Today, you can ferret out cards if you want to take the time and trouble to go to small towns. It requires a great amount of skill, patience, and subtle bargaining strategy, so you'll want to try this on a limited basis, if at all. Say you're taking a two-week vacation trip, for example. Place a classified ad in the area's local papers saying you're buying cards and memorabilia on a certain date, and leave your local phone number.

When you find yourself in any new locale, you should also check with the local courthouse or post office to find whether there were any five-and-dime stores, candy stores, or distributors that recently retired and closed up shop. Often, these people have cartons of baseball material accumulated over the years that didn't sell. Don't be shy about knocking on someone's door if you get a lead. Of course, if there's already a baseball card shop in town, your chances are next to nil that any cache hasn't yet been uncovered. But in small rural areas, you can run your own one-man convention. Tack up signs and put them in the supermarket. Print fliers and gossip with the guy who owns the coffee shop.

Imagination is critical here. Let's say you find yourself in Ohio. If you check the *Baseball Encyclopedia,* you can scan the famous players and look for their birth and death locales. Cy Young, for instance, was born in Gilmore, Ohio, and died in Newcomerstown, Ohio. Does any Cy Young memorabilia exist in either place? Who knows? Even though Young died in 1955, there's still a chance some of the townsfolk latched onto some piece of the great pitcher's career. Collectors lusted after Lou Gehrig's high school yearbook, even in so-so condition. I'd love to know if there are any schoolboy artifacts of Cy Young.

Let's say you find someone looking to sell a card collection. He'll expect a fair market value offer, but he hasn't taken the initiative to begin calling dealers. Or, for some reason or another, he's reluctant to let them out of his home for appraisal. Of course, you'll have to bring a current price guide.

MR. MINT'S MAXIM: *Dealers are willing to pay 60 to 70 percent of book value for cards in top condition made before 1980. (Very old, scarce cards are often bought at 100 percent of book value, or more.) If you're buying from a private collector, you'll want to pay less than retail, and he'll want to sell for more than wholesale, or roughly a dealer's buy price. So a good starting point of negotiation might be slightly higher than 60 percent of book value.*

Suppose the seller is using the SCD Pocket Price Guide, and you have Beckett's guide. Naturally, there will be disparities on certain cards, especially those with high value. The obvious method of compromise is to split the difference. For example, suppose he has a 1962 Roger Maris card in near mint condition. It lists for $150 in your guide, and $175 in his. You might say, "Let's use $162 as the middle." A dealer would offer about $100. Offer to pay that. If he balks, you can go to $115 (which is 70 percent of book), and still get an excellent deal.

Of course, you can use the same negotiation strategy with any collector who has cards you want. Remember, collectors are finicky, and you're not likely to exercise any bargaining might over people who have no vested interest in selling. Often the people you meet in the hobby are more inclined to want to trade for something they want. In that case, you both must first agree to what is the fair market value of the items involved.

Assume, for instance, that you did pick up that Roger Maris card from a far-flung collector who was willing to sell it. On your next stop, you ran into a coin and baseball card shop dealer in eastern Long Island in a resort town. You look through the glass display cases and inspect his wares. He's a retailer with a hefty overhead, so none of his star cards are being offered at any bargain prices. Most of the shop owners, when they're not busy, love to talk baseball, so you strike up a conversation. You find that you're both Mets fans. He has an interesting item not on display that he'd like to show you. It's an undated metal printer's proof sheet from 1969, with the *New York Times* logo at the top of the page. It's a "negative" sheet (meaning everything is backward, or mirror-imaged), and you see that it has pictures of the entire world champion Mets team with capsule summaries of the players' season. The dealer explains that it's probably a one-of-a-kind item, and since it was undated, it probably was printed in a Sunday supplement. It might have been a reject, never published. He had no idea what to offer the youth who came in with it. Seventy-five dollars was mentioned by the seller. Finally, the seller said, would you give me $100 in a trade? The dealer said sure. So the kid took a set of cards worth $105 and gave up the printer's sheet.

Now the dealer's into it for $105 retail, and he likes it enough to keep it. You offer $175 because you know a bunch of Mets fanatics back in Queens who would easily pay $250 or $300. The dealer balks, even at a quick profit of 70 percent on his money. You might offer more, but since there's no "book" on this item, you don't want to overpay either.

Here's where creativity and nerves come in. You suddenly ask, "Would you have a need for a 1962 Roger Maris card in near mint condition?" The dealer happens to know someone looking for that card, and he asks you to bring it in. You tell him you bought it for $110. He knows a 1960s Yankees collector whom he just sold a single-signed Maris ball who's been looking for such a card for a long time. He's seen a lot of off-condition cards, but he'll gladly pay upwards of $200 for a great example. When you walk in with the near mint Maris, his eyes gleam. Offer him a straight-up trade. If he says no, sweeten the offer with a $10 or $20 bill.

Now let's examine what's happened, or could have happened,

since this is a fictional scenario. The dealer ended up with a card he will immediately turn over for a $50 or $100 profit over the Mets sheet, but his real profit was likely to be a lot more. The cards he originally let go in a trade he probably bought for far less than the $105 value he placed on it (remember, it was retail, not wholesale). You paid $115 for the Maris card, but you now own the Mets sheet for $115 (plus the sweetener, say $20). Your investment is only $135 for an item you will easily get $200 for in a Queens card shop. Or, if you're enterprising and shop it around a bit, perhaps $50 or $100 more from an avid Mets collector.

MR. MINT'S MAXIM: *It's extremely difficult to find any worthwhile buys at the local card shop (at least until you get to know the owner well). Do not be surprised to discover that most small stores generally have very high prices—sometimes as much as 15 to 20 percent or more above the current prices quoted in the weekly SCD listings. Consequently, their buy prices are extremely low, too.*

Much of the time, there are tangible reasons why the card shop owner's prices are high. He is often dealing in the current player market, and kids are his major market. Some set has gotten hot because a player has had a great season. He was into it a few years ago for the wholesale price, and now he wants to cash in a big profit. In 1990, for example, Ryne Sandberg, the Cubs marvelous second baseman, finally caught on with collectors as being a "career" talent. Two months into the season, his 1983 Topps rookie card was selling for $15 to $20. Just after the All-Star break Sandberg's card was retailing for $40 to $50, and the 1983 Topps complete set had shot up to $120 from about $85, a 40 percent increase in a matter of weeks.

But the economics of the small retailer won't hold any promise for those of you trying to buy and sell cards for a profit. Besides the usual overhead expenses that keep his prices high, you're still dealing with a personality that has more than a little collector left in him. He may keep items in his window that are not for sale at any price, and that is a singular indication that he won't be negotiable on much of his quality merchandise. I hope the card shop owners don't think I'm trying to berate small businessmen here. I'm not. There are some very smart guys out there running stores, and they know how to do business. If you're lucky enough to live near one of these fellows, then you're likely to forge an equitable buy–sell relationship that has a chance to flourish and be profitable.

I'm still constantly amazed that 90 percent of the baseball card and memorabilia dealers I run into are not very knowledgeable or professional. It's difficult or impossible to do business with them. The local guy tends to mark up an item 50 to 100 percent the day after he buys it. If it languishes in the display case for a year or more, this dealer will wait it out until he gets his price. He probably doesn't understand the time element of the business; he'd prefer to make 100 percent profit in a year (and that is not at all sure) rather than a guaranteed 10 percent profit in a day. The typical mom-and-pop operation has a lingering streak of the collector in it, an unrequited love of maintaining a big inventory. If I were to walk into this kind of store and offer a fantastic price for everything in it—cash, on the spot—the odds are it would be summarily turned down. Why? There would be nothing to sell in the morning. Whereas a smart retailer would close up shop and make a two-week buying trip to someplace where he knows he can replenish the cards in his glass cases. He would have confidence that he could turn over the money again, and that every time he does it he'll turn a profit.

It's just as likely the retailer does understand the basic economic equations and prefers to ignore them, either because he's plain stubborn or because there's just not enough product out there to acquire. Remember, most card shop owners don't travel to shows, because they're too busy minding their stores. I met one guy, a dealer, who has hundreds of cases of unopened wax boxes, hundreds of complete mint sets, all sitting in his garage. He won't budge on prices, because he doesn't need the money. And some stuff he wouldn't sell at any price—he would only give them up on a trade. There's nothing wrong with these folks; in fact, they may be the only godsends left in the hobby. But they're like rocks. You'll have a tough time doing any business with them.

Still, make it a point to become a fixture at your local dealer, for two important reasons: One, he loves to talk about the hobby, and two, he's likely to hear rumors—which, for good or bad, are an integral influence on the price of many items—far earlier than you'll read about them in SCD. The hobby store is a generous cracker barrel for gaining investment knowledge and learning how to spot price trends.

The other reason to hang out at the store is that you'll meet other collectors. And that's an important means to making better buying and selling connections.

I know two beginning collectors who happened to meet at a New York City card store they both deemed ridiculously overpriced, even though it was situated in a neighborhood with reasonable commercial rents. One guy overheard the other making an unsuccessful attempt to get the retailer to lower his price on an autographed bat that was widely available at a significantly lower price through mail order in SCD. The dealer refused to come down a nickel. The other had had the same experience with the dealer, and the two introduced themselves at the door. When they got to know each other, they found they were of roughly the same vintage (they were in their 40s, and both spent their boyhood tracking the Dodgers, Giants, and Yankees of the 1950s and 1960s). They had similar but not essentially the same collecting interests. Both collected Hall of Fame balls, but one guy loved cards, and the other wouldn't touch them. The guy who wouldn't touch cards collected autographed 8″ by 10″ glossies. The card guy couldn't have cared less about signed pictures. But they began traveling to shows together, shared information, and they kept each other apprised when they spotted bargains the other person might be interested in. Word of mouth can travel a long way.

After you're familiar with SCD and the general price range of certain cards, you'll wonder about buying through mail order, since this is by far the way most business is done. It's difficult to recommend making a purchase, especially a substantial one in four figures, without first inspecting the goods. Though SCD's advertising staff does its best to weed out unreliable and dishonest dealers, you're always taking a chance when ordering through the mail unless you've checked the dealer's credentials in advance. If you're going to shop this way, it's a good idea to call SCD and ask if there have been customer complaints in the files of a given dealer.

MR. MINT'S MAXIM: *Get to know a dealer in person first, if possible, before you call him on the phone and make a buy without seeing the cards. Make certain he has a well-defined and liberal return policy if you're unhappy with what you've bought.*

Perhaps the easiest place to do business, as well as meet other collectors and dealers, is at the great American card shows, which have become fixtures all over the United States in recent years. Card shows, as you probably suspected, come in all shapes and sizes, from the massive National Convention, which attracts the biggest dealers and crowds once a year on the long July 4 weekend, to the tiny 10-table show at a small church or Holiday Inn on a Thursday night. Admission charges vary, but it's safe to say that most small shows let you in gratis or for a dollar, and charge modest rental fees for dealer tables, $20 to $50. More extensive and widely advertised shows have higher up-front costs, so you're likely to pay an admission charge of $4 or $5 a day. Dealers pay table rentals of $100 to $250.

In every issue SCD lists between 300 and 500 shows across North America, from Alabama to Canada, in any given two-week period. Start by attending those close to home, or those you can drive to for a weekend. After you've exhausted the local shows (and this you will do rather quickly), you'll want to travel to more substantial card conventions. Those with more than 100 dealer tables are usually advertised in local papers or the SCD, and will often have one or more current or retired baseball personalities on hand to sign autographs.

MR. MINT'S MAXIM: *The autograph lines for baseball stars are for your kids, not for serious investors. Promoters have autograph signings to build the gate; rarely do they pay off, because the more expensive marquee players (Mays, Mantle, DiMaggio, to name the three most visible) are becoming more and more cost-prohibitive. Promoters must pay the big names anywhere from $15,000 to $25,000 and up for an afternoon's work of signing. The charge is usually $30 to $45 per autograph for the biggest legends of the game. Also, more and more stars are refusing to sign bats and balls, or anything other than a "flat item."*

Avoid the autograph-line syndrome. You'll save a lot of wear on your legs, not to mention time.

Here is a typical story that will illustrate the trap of waiting on line for autographs. A New York collector wanted to get an autographed ball with Mays, Mantle, and Duke Snider. At one time these three great center fielders were among the best who ever roamed the outfield, and, of course, they all played for New York area teams at the same time. This collector bought an official ball for $6 at a sporting goods store and traveled to a show where Mays was signing autographs. Mays signed on the "sweet spot," or the "manager's spot"—the narrowest space between the seams—for $25. The collector took the ball to another show where Mantle was signing. He procured the Mick's signature for $35. Snider proved to be a bit more elusive, but the collector eventually found a show where the Duke was signing in Somerset, New Jersey. But he couldn't attend that weekend. Luckily, the show's promoters accepted mail-order items for autographs. The promoters only charged $14 for Snider's signature, but he had to add $10 for postage and insurance and another $4 to get it returned. Astute readers will note that our brilliant collector was now into this ball for $94, plus all the time on line, and money spent for transportation to and from the Mays and Mantle shows.

I offered the same triple-signature ball for sale (with Mantle on the sweet spot, which is more desirable than his ball) by mail order for $125, postpaid. Even though this collector justified his behavior by the combination thrill of the hunt and the 15-second encounter with two of his childhood heroes, he realized he'd made a foolish use of his time and energy to save $31.

But the card shows themselves are the lifeblood of a good deal of the baseball card business, and the more you can attend them, the more current you'll be in the hobby.

You'll notice several things right away at card shows that differ from your local card store. First, you have a much wider selection of products. The dealer may own a store where his customers are more captive, but now he is in a highly competitive situation. He knows that any customer, if he doesn't like his merchandise, can shop at dozens of outlets a few yards away.

MR. MINT'S MAXIM: *Nobody pays full retail at a card show, or at least nobody has to. Dealers are fully aware that a show often favors a buyer's market. The smarter ones are willing to horse-trade and grant liberal discounts, especially to quantity buyers with cash.*

Second, the level of wheeling and dealing can often occur at astonishing speed. Dealers are keenly on the lookout for the guy who is unloading a run of Topps sets from 1965 to 1974, and they'll hone in on him like a shark circling a swimmer with a bloody toe. The average showgoer doesn't know it, but many of these collections are bought and sold three and four times over a weekend. Since my philosophy is to flip collections as quickly as possible, I most often function as a wholesaler, buying from individuals and selling to dealers.

MR. MINT'S MAXIM: *Get to know the biggest dealers at shows, because they carry the highest-quality items and work on the smallest margins. You can find them by asking other knowledgeable collectors. Also, they're likely to hold their wares for the shortest period of time and often replenish their stock in hours.*

A new collector I know wanted to accumulate a couple of sets in a short period of time. He knew he'd have to temper the urge to immediately begin buying expensive cards. It's prudent to be tentative in the beginning. Rather than start throwing several thousand dollars into cards, he wanted to invest a few hundred dollars at a time. He began pricing sets at card shows, and eventually he met a Pennsylvania dealer who always brought 10 to 15 sets of top-grade cards to shows.

The key for him was that this dealer always seemed to sell out immediately. The show would open on Friday night, and by Saturday morning this dealer had already crossed off half the sets on the cardboard sign listing his wares.

As the collector gained confidence, he spotted his first buy, a 1980 Topps set which was booking in 1990 for $175 to $200 in near mint to mint condition. The Rickey Henderson rookie card was kept separately in a plastic holder (at $125 it is the single card that drives the value of the set). The Henderson card was perfect, and the buyer offered $160 cash. The dealer accepted. This new collector knew that when Henderson broke Ty Cobb's all-time base-stealing record, the milestone would be sure to juice the price of the card. He could easily sell the set for $200 in two months for a 25 percent return on his investment. Not a killing by any means, but a good start, and certainly better than any money market account.

Now, the dealer might have been able to get his $185 asking price by Sunday afternoon, but he was willing to take a smaller, certain profit right away. He also sent a message to the collector that he was both flexible and trustworthy. He was thinking of repeat business. When the collector investigated the prices of other sets—all Topps sets between 1975 and the present—he carefully noted prices listed in the ads and weekly guides in SCD. Before he made a move, he called the Pennsylvania dealer and asked for a quote. He ended up buying six more sets, two of which were slightly below the current SCD weekly price guide report.

MR. MINT'S MAXIM: *There are dealers who are part-timers who merely want to show off their collections. These "weekend warriors" attend card shows only to amuse themselves and are rock-hard when it comes to bargaining. You can spot them by their never-changing inventories and the dearth of customers at their booths. Don't bother with them. They're not interested in selling unless you're willing to pay their outlandishly high prices.*

Despite the chaotic, bazaarlike atmosphere at large shows, there is a logical method of shopping for cards and other collectibles, whether you know what you're looking for, or whether you're on a general prowl. Timing, of course, can sometimes make a big difference in price, even over the course of a weekend, so you should know when to shop. The big shows usually begin on Friday evenings and end on Sunday afternoons. Saturday afternoons, often when the star autographer is present, usually generate the largest amount of customer traffic. It's commonly thought that the best bargains exist just when the show closes, when a dealer may not have done enough business to pay for his table rental, hotel room, and other expenses. Similar logic dictates that he doesn't want to lug home all those boxes of unsold cards.

MR. MINT'S MAXIM: *You are better off looking for a buy just when the show opens, when dealers themselves often do not know what items will be in buyer demand. Also, smart dealers often know their first offer on a particular item is the best (or only) one they'll get that weekend.*

This doesn't mean you buy that great-looking card at the first table you stop at as soon as the doors of the show open. You may end up buying that card, but not until you scour every table that might contain a duplicate. Let's use a reasonably priced card as an example, Carlton Fisk's 1972 Topps rookie card, #79, which he shares with Cecil Cooper and Mike Garman. The price guides tell you that the card has been selling anywhere from $75 to $100. You carry a notepad with you, and take the next 15 minutes to ask the dealers who carry rookie cards whether they have a Fisk. Do not forget to ask; most adept dealers do not display everything they bring. Note the condition, the booth location, and the asking price on every Fisk card in the show. Let's say you find eight different cards, ranging from very good at $40 up to a perfectly centered, gem mint one for $150. There are two near mint cards for $125 offered by one dealer.

What do you do?

First, as we discussed in the last chapter on condition, you eliminate every one but the near mint or mint cards. My suggestion would be to ask the dealer with the two near mint cards if he'd take $200 for both. If not, try the one with the perfect card; offer $125. If neither guy budges, then buy the great card for $150, anyway. (Chances are that one will be flexible, especially when you casually mention that somebody else has a nice one you're considering.) You will not have made an error even though you've just paid the highest price for a Fisk rookie card at the show. Here's why: One, Pudge's card has plenty of upside. He is one of baseball's most durable catchers, having played 21 seasons, half with the Red Sox, half with the White Sox. He's 42 years old, and he'll likely be hanging up his spikes soon. Catchers are underrepresented in the Hall of Fame (try naming five as an exercise: Dickey, Hartnett, Campanella, Berra, Bench; see—I told you, it's not so easy) and Fisk with 336 homers and a lifetime batting average of .271 has a better than average change of getting elected. This makes the long-term investment possibilities of this card excellent.

I'd like to end this chapter by offering one piece of advice for all those collector/investors who are prone to impulse buys on cards and items available in extraordinary places.

MR. MINT'S MAXIM: *Resist the urge to shop for a card at a store like Macy's, which, for instance, has a card counter next to the bridal registry in one of its stores. These outlets merely serve the casual buyer or the person looking for a gift for a collector. The prices are high, usually higher than retail.*

One final warning for all those readers who subscribe to cable television: One day, you will be flipping through the channels and you'll see a woman's hand gently caress the signed plaque of a famous major league player. Perhaps you'll even see the likes of Henry Aaron flogging his wares in person. A satisfied buyer/caller will be enthusiastically chirping about the profit he made on the autographed bat he bought.

The announcer will tell you the remaining items are going fast, and at incredibly reduced prices, so hurry and dial, and have your credit card number handy. Do not be seduced. Do not get near a telephone. You will be paying a premium that is far higher for the exact merchandise found at any card show or through the many ads in the trade papers.

Do not shop for baseball memorabilia on the Home Shopping Network. Memorize that bit of advice and you will have paid for the price of this book with your first purchase.

Do not worry about passing up a card that you fear you'll never find again. If a nonbaseball card specialty outlet has it, and the proprietor knows it's a special card, he'll be even more resistant to bargaining and lowering the price. It will appear again, in some other locale.

SHOULD YOU INVEST
IN COMPLETE SETS?

One of the most common questions asked by newcomers to the baseball card business is, "Should I invest in complete sets?" The answer is emphatically yes on sets 1975 and earlier, and a cautious, qualified yes on sets from 1976 on. Be especially aware that anytime you're buying sets manufactured in the last eight to ten years the scarcity factor will have little influence in the market. (*Perceived* scarcity, however, is another matter. When collectors merely think a set is difficult to find, the price is higher than it normally should be.) Remember, the companies have made millions and millions more cards than they did before the business boomed in the 1980s. Demand alone is the driving force for the buy-sell prices of these late sets.

In an effort to illustrate what not to do, bear with me while I recount one of my more horrendous investments.

Back in 1987, I decided to take a flier on the special Fleer Update set. An "update" or "traded" set is produced by the card companies later in a given year to reflect the trades and new rookies who've been called up to their major-league clubs. But Fleer issued a classier limited edition of cards that were plastic-coated and sealed in tin. They were known as the "glossy tin" sets.

While the set was lovingly produced, Fleer did not specifically define what it meant by "limited" production in this 132-card issue. Well, the $19 wholesale price shot up quickly to $99, and there were all sorts of sell ads in SCD. So I decided to place a buy ad. I wanted to get as many as I could at $60 a set. I contracted to buy 800 sets, in two 400-set lots, for $48,000 from a dealer in Kansas City. I took delivery on the first 400 sets. I sold some, but not many, perhaps 50 or 75 sets, at $99. But then, as word filtered out that Fleer had actually produced as many as 75,000 to 100,000 of the tin glossies, the market began plummeting. I quickly tried to recover by wholesaling them in quantity for $70 a set, then $61 a set, just to get out and cut my losses. The country was glutted with them, and soon all the dealers who bought in at $19 a set were profit-taking, just like the stock market. Soon, they had dropped to around $30 apiece again, the same price as Fleer's standard update set, minus $30 each, as far as I was concerned.

The guy in Kansas City, naturally, phoned me to ship the other 400 sets, and since I'd given my word, I paid $60 apiece, even though I still had 50 or so left from the original delivery. I kept the 450 sets for some time, and then I finally unloaded them at $35 and a net loss that was so disturbing and embarrassing I'll let you tally it up.

This is known as speculating, not investing, and I paid dearly for the privilege.

MR. MINT'S MAXIM: *If you're going to invest in "current" complete sets of cards, you must buy in large quantities at a substantial discount. Buy wholesale only, or close to the wholesale price.*

A few years ago, I bought 5,000 sets of 1987 Topps cards, and 5,000 sets of 1988s. The buy price was $14 a set, which was wholesale. Remember, you do not need to be a dealer to place a buy ad in SCD. The distributor who sold them cared only that I had the $70,000. Although this looked risky, it was not. The sets will never be worth less than $14 apiece, so I have a very limited downside. Only a really flat economy could ever cause a "loss" by less than anticipated growth over a period of time. Buying these cards is like an annuity for me. I waited for the cards to mature slightly, and when I began seeing sell prices rise in the SCD last year ($25 to $30 for the 1987 sets, and $20 to $25 for the 1988s), I offered my sets at $27 and $21 respectively. Anyone who knows how I work could call and get quantity price quotes. I'm now willing to begin taking a profit, and my sell price is probably lower than anyone else's. The sets I don't sell will continue to appreciate at modest levels every year.

Obviously, this was a far more intelligent market play than my 1987 tin glossy Fleer set escapade.

In 1975 Topps released a special "mini" set of its regular run, and test-marketed them in certain areas of the country. The cards were no different from the large-sized cards, but immediately collectors assumed they were rare and had a special cachet. The experiment was a dud because Topps chose not to repeat it. (One reason was the cards didn't fit properly in plastic holders, and they jostled around in the conventionally sized boxes. Collectors like things neat and orderly.) When the 1975 cards began increasing in value, the minis went up to almost double the price of the normal-sized cards. At one time a 1975 set was $300 and the mini was $600. But then an interesting thing happened in the late 1980s. Collectors decided they weren't so desirable after all, and they no longer escalated at the same rate as the larger counterpart. Demand decreased and dealers were forced to respond by lowering their prices. When the regular set reached $700, the mini was not $1,400 but only $1,000. The minis were a spectacular investment only if you bought in low when they were issued and unloaded them precisely at the peak market. But who knew what the peak was?

For the long run, a collector would have done better in the safer, regular-sized set of cards. Today, the demand for minis is much lower than it was, even though they're harder by far to find than a set of normal 1975s.

MR. MINT'S MAXIM: *With few exceptions, the gimmick sets are bad long-term investments. The market will make huge swings overnight and may be impossible to predict. Be very skeptical of sudden and very steep price rises on any one- or two-year-old issue. If you see an Upper Deck set issued at $40 immediately jump to $75, caveat emptor. It's just as likely to drop after you buy them because they're suddenly "available."*

Do not expect any consistency in price increase or fluctuation on any sets made in the last few years, especially since there's already some discussion as to what constitutes a true "mint" set. Let's take the 1991 issues (it doesn't matter whether they're Topps, Fleer, Score, or Donruss). You've breezed through three or four shows, and you've been somewhat mystified by one of card collecting's characteristically illogical situations. The prices for current sets vary a dollar or two from table to table (many dealers will take only the smallest profits, using them as a loss leader). But the Topps complete sets, for instance, come in two different mint varieties: the "factory-sealed" boxes at $23 to $26 apiece and the "hand-collated" boxes at less—$20 to $22.

You ask a few dealers about this, and they tell you that the sets assembled by hand actually contain a "better overall" condition than the factory-sealed sets. So, a dealer claims, any card that isn't properly centered or has a printing defect is thrown out. The dealer paid very low wages to high school kids and part-time help to assemble the sets in order, from card number 1 to 792 from the factory cases he bought. Well, if that's the case, why don't they charge more for them than the factory issue? How could a handmade anything cost less than the equivalent mass-produced version? you're wondering. The prices are lower because he bought in such large quantity that he was able to assemble the sets for less than the factory wholesale price. As someone who is well acquainted with the numbers, this seems to me like a fairy tale. I cannot see how dealers make a reasonable profit by doing this.

Even if I'm wrong, do not buy the less expensive hand-collated sets (well, buy one so you have cards to flip and abuse with your kids). Pay a few extra dollars to get the factory sets and leave them unopened. When it's time to sell them, the sealed cases will still be worth more and probably increase at a greater rate than the hand-assembled sets. Do not worry that your factory cards aren't in numerical order. Do not worry that dealers will warn you that there's a chance the star cards are miscut or off center. And especially do not worry if a dealer says, "How do you know what's in there if you don't open it?" Well, if the factory cases contain bricks instead of cards, then the hobby as well as the business is in serious trouble.

MR. MINT'S MAXIM: *If you're going to take a big position on several dozen sets of current cards, do not buy them at the beginning of the season. Wait until the end of the year, when every dealer is looking to dump his unsold inventory. They have to generate cash to buy next year's new product. In January, everyone is asking full retail for the upcoming season's sets. By October or November, when the card companies are sending out order forms for 1992, that's when to buy the 1991s in bulk.*

Still, remember that this kind of investing is more of a commodities brokerage game, and it's drifting away from the established staples of antique cards. Think of it this way. Instead of buying a long-established blue chip stock, you're taking a chance on a new low-priced issue, an unproven company. The irrefutable history of baseball cards still dictates that the older the set you buy, the safer the risk.

From 1952 to 1973, when Topps was essentially the only card manufacturer in the business, cards appeared each season in "series." That means the cards were manufactured in chunks and released periodically throughout the season. For instance, in 1970, there were six series (numbers 1–132, 133–263, 264–459, 460–546, 547–633, and 634–720). By 1973, there were only four series issued, and the following year, Topps began selling every single card all at one time, a practice that has survived today and is followed by virtually all the card companies. When you check the price guides, you'll note that the later series, or the high-numbered cards, usually are more difficult to find, and hence cost more on an across-the-board basis. This is because as the baseball season grew into late summer and fall, and card sales began slowing, candy stores began stocking football cards and other items. (Occasionally, you'll see a second or third series that is scarcer than the high-numbered series. The price guides indicate scarcity by the price quotes of the common cards.) Though the 1974 and 1975 cards were issued all at once, they were not sold in complete sets, so they are difficult to find in top-quality condition. Bear in mind, too, that Topps did not sell complete factory sets until many years later.

In my opinion, if you pay full retail, or even slightly higher than book value, on near mint sets prior to and through 1975, it is virtually impossible to make a mistake. You will get ample return on any of these sets (some are better than others, however, and you should read Chapter 13 for my picks for the 1990s for specific advice on sets).

For example, let's say you have a chance to buy either a single near mint 1975 Topps set at $750 or four 1980 Topps sets at $200 each, with a $50 discount ($750 for the four). What do you do? The 1980 set has the Rickey Henderson rookie card, which in 1990 seemed to be soaring like IBM in a bull market. But the 1975 has the rookie cards of Robin Yount, George Brett, Jim Rice, Gary Carter, Fred Lynn, and Keith Hernandez. Even if Rickey Henderson is a 95 percent certain Hall of Famer (and Yount and Brett are, say, 75 percent certain), you should buy the single 1975 set. In fact, the Hall of Fame candidacy of the star rookie cards is less important than the availability of the sets. The 1975 is simply much scarcer than the 1980, when thousands of collectors began putting complete sets away in their closets. It's also five years older, and people will always desire something older than newer in this business.

If you have less money to invest and want to buy complete sets from 1980 to the present, there is nothing wrong with this philosophy. Just remember that you are not alone, and you'll have to be patient. You probably will be competing with dealers like myself who are stockpiling them, waiting for a hot rookie to juice the price of the set. Do not expect to turn these sets over very quickly for a profit. Consider them more like individual retirement accounts; you'll likely cash in and make a profit, but not until several years from now. The annual rate of return will probably exceed the 7 or 8 percent you're getting from a conservative financial instrument offered by a broker.

If you wanted to buy, say, five sets of the current 1991 issue, is it better to buy one each of Upper Deck, Score, Fleer, Tops, and Donruss, or should you buy five of the set you think has the greatest growth potential? A few years ago, I might have said just buy five Topps sets. But now the other companies are just as good as, if not better than, Topps at predicting next season's stars. Also, collectors correctly perceive that the other companies have competed heavily and successfully on aesthetics with Topps. Their cards are usually just as nice or nicer, even though Topps has managed to lead the country in name recognition. The 1987 Fleer is worth roughly triple what the 1987 Topps is worth, mainly because Fleer has a nicer set. They both contain virtually the same star cards. In 1984, Fleer's set only contained 660 cards, while Topps printed 792 cards. Yet the Fleer books for about 1½ times what the Topps set lists for.

While you're pondering just where to make your first complete set investment, your brain is no doubt inundated with the hundreds of pages of ads hawking bulk "rookie" specials of current players. (There are few good reasons why the concept of a rookie or first card is more desirable from the pure fan's standpoint. Mickey Mantle's first card shows all the boyhood promise of the superstar-to-be—there's no doubt it's a beautiful card—but his 1969 card, his swan song, contains all the stats of his career on the back. For me, and other true baseball fans, I suspect it's a lot more interesting reading.)

In 1990, the preseason names bandied about were John Olerud, Ben MacDonald, Steve Avery, Sandy Alomar, Jr., Todd Zeile, and Juan Gonzalez. Some of these cards were trading for $1 to $2 even before the players had been called up from the minors. Juan Gonzalez, for example, was listed in a midsummer SCD price guide at 40 cents for his Topps cards, and $1 for the Upper Deck card. Gonzalez, a top prospect for the Texas Rangers outfield, had been burning up Triple A in Oklahoma City. But as of the first of August, he hadn't yet been brought up to the major leagues. (He did make his debut late in the 1990 season, and he showed a lot of potential.)

There are hundreds of ads each week in SCD where dealers are blowing out huge quantities of these hot rookies, and it's mesmerizing to imagine that people are putting a hundred dollars or more into the future of a Steve Avery. I call this the slot-machine theory of investing. It's a lot like going to Las Vegas and pulling the lever of a one-arm bandit, dreaming of a big score.

If you follow this route, you are headed down the road to disaster. You have a 1 in 20 chance of hitting. What percentage of each year's crop of rookies become journeyman players? What percentage become stars or superstars? Remember Joe Charboneau? Of course you don't. In 1980 the 25-year-old Cleveland outfielder hit 23 homers and won Rookie of the Year honors. His card was red-hot, selling for a few dollars each. Two years later, he had dyed his hair red and was out of baseball.

Today, his 1981 Topps rookie card can be purchased for 12 cents.

I belabor this point to convince you how volatile the current rookie market is and how impossibly frustrating it is to predict, no matter how close you study it. Major-league teams general managers earn far more money than most people just to ponder this question. It is very easy to get sucked into buying these cards in 100- or 1,000-card lots on the basis of one season or less. So don't do it, not even if you're related to someone you think will be the next Jose Canseco. *Baseball America,* the newspaper that covers the minor leagues, is an excellent source of information on upcoming stars, but it is very often wrong. It only reports on players with potential who have shown talent in the minor leagues. Its crystal ball is no more reliable than any good general manager or scout.

If you're still not convinced, let me offer another example of how headstrong I was about this gamble at one time. Back in 1982, Dave Righetti was the heralded rookie starting pitcher for the Yankees, and he jumped out to a 4-0 start. I figured Rags' card couldn't miss, so I invested $7,500 in him (10,000 cards at 75 cents apiece). That was a lot less than Steinbrenner's risk, but it was a lot of faith on my part based on just a few weeks in the majors. The day after I bought the cards, disaster struck. Righetti lost four or five games in a row, or something like that. Suddenly, he couldn't get anybody out. He ended up being sent to the minor leagues for further schooling, and today his card is still selling at about the same price I paid nine years ago. You can easily calculate the lost interest on that investment. The money would have been better invested in a savings account. I like Righetti, and I'm still a lifelong Yankee's fan, but he taught me a tough lesson. And I swear that's the last current rookie investment I'll ever make.

Yes, I should have known better. I've been successful in every phase of this business except guessing and gambling. Do not guess. Do not gamble.

I do not mean to snicker at the faithful collectors and investors who have dozens of Don Mattingly rookie cards, and those others who bought in much later at $25 to $50 apiece. But the handwriting was on the wall long before his back injury caused a slump and his missing the second half of the 1990 season. Prior to 1990 many baseball pundits had noted that his power outage had fallen considerably; his line drives had lost their punch, and fewer were going out of the park. His effortless, smooth hitting stroke was harmed by the back injury long before it became public. I attribute this to the fact that Mattingly is a classy athlete, and he doesn't stay home simply because of a little nagging ache. Unfortunately, this little nagging ache is now a major one.

But the cold, cruel fact is that a bad back is bad for the price of his card. Mattingly's career, despite a .323 lifetime batting average and the fact that he has won an MVP award, is in decline. Still, you will see ludicrous ads in SCD promoting Mattingly merchandise, claiming that he's a future Hall of Famer.

Bret Saberhagen is another example. Sure, he has two Cy Young Awards under him, and that's quite an accomplishment for the young Kansas City hurler. But his first four seasons were so erratic, the price of his rookie card went from $1 to $5, back to $1, back up to $5, then down to $2. What does this mean? Simply that Saberhagen is a bad investment for a baseball card collector and still an unproven talent for the long run.

MR. MINT'S MAXIM: *Do not buy into Jose Canseco futures, no matter how many home runs you think he's going to hit. It is too early to tell whether he'll be the next Mickey Mantle. Nobody wishes any bad luck or ill harm to one of baseball's brightest talents, but if he gets arrested for gun possession or wraps a sports car around a tree and his career ends, then all those Canseco rookie cards will never be worth what you paid. One other reason: The scarcity of Mantle cards* *is fairly well known. In 40 years when Canseco is an old geezer signing autographs at shows, collectors will pull out his rookie cards by the wagonload. There are just too many of his cards being hoarded.*

There is another anomaly in the logic of price on baseball cards, and you may have noticed this when you've browsed through the price guides on older sets. The sum of the individual cards in a given set is always greater than the price of the complete set. In other words, if you were to buy each card, one at a time, it would cost you far more than if you bought the set outright. The reason for this is that the market for star cards is very strong, and often collectors would prefer having seven or eight players from a given set rather than the hundreds of common cards. If you wanted to sell a complete set a card at a time, it would take somewhere between a long time and forever. However, you still might not reap a greater amount of money or profit if you had sold the complete set. Why? It's not easy to find a buyer at $3 or $4 for a 1969 Jim Bunning card, or $10 for a Don Money rookie card. There is a strong market for Willie Mays, Carl Yazstremski, and Hank Aaron from that series, however, and you'd easily sell those.

MR. MINT'S MAXIM: *You cannot lose money buying a complete set, but you can lose by buying a single card, especially if the player is currently active.*

Now, let's suppose you have a chance to buy a complete set of 1972 Topps cards. The seller is a collector who painstakingly assembled the cards over a period of time, not necessarily one by one, but in pieces. It took him a very long time, he says, to find the high-numbered cards in near mint condition, but he did. Book value of this set in top condition is $1,500, but he's willing to let it go for the bargain price of only $1,000.

Why so low? you wonder. He notices your surprise, and because he's honest and doesn't want to deceive anyone, he explains that the key cards in the set—the Carlton Fisk rookie, the Nolan Ryan, and the Rod Carew—grade only excellent to near mint. You check those cards and they look okay, but some of the corners on all three cards are slightly worn.

You flick through the rest of the set and they're all near mint, just as he said.

Should you buy this set? No, because when it comes time to sell, you're stuck with the incontrovertible reality that the set as a *whole* is off condition, even if it's only three cards. When it comes time to sell, you will be stuck reciting the same litany to the buyer that you just heard. You could buy the set for $1,000 and then upgrade the three star cards. But what do you think that might cost? You check the guide and see the total was at least $350 to $400 for those cards. Trust me, it will cost at least $500 or more to get those three cards in near mint to mint condition. In order to upgrade the total value of the set, your investment will most likely exceed the total cost of a near mint set.

Should you construe my sermon in this chapter to mean that you should never buy an individual baseball card? Of course not. There are many excellent investments in name players. I'll explain who they are in a later chapter.

NEW YORK SYNDROME
OR, THE MICKEY MANTLE AURA

Roger Clemens' 1985 Topps rookie card was issued in roughly the same numbers as Dave Stewart's 1982 Topps rookie card. Their pitching talent is remarkably equal and they're arguably the two most talented starters in the game today. Clemens has two Cy Young Awards and an MVP, and Stewart has four consecutive 20-game win seasons and a World Series MVP. (Granted, when they face each other, Stewart seems to beat Clemens almost every time.) Both men, incidentally, come across through the media as reasonably intelligent, affable personalities. Maybe not yet heroes, but the kinds of guys kids can look up to. Clemens plays in Boston, and Stewart in Oakland, two good franchises, two cities with lots of collectors. Clemens is a great role model for Boston's white youth, and Stewart sets a wonderful example for inner-city black kids not only in the Bay Area but across the nation.

All things in the Clemens-Stewart comparison being on parity, their cards should be selling for about the same amount. Yet Clemens' card is $15 to $18, more than twice Stewart's, which books for $6 plus. A lot of right-thinking, liberal people hope that in the future the cards of the Dave Stewarts of the baseball world will begin to catch up with the Roger Clemenses. But, to borrow from a Damon Runyon saying, that is not the way to bet. Buyer demand favors Clemens by a wide margin.

Few institutions in this world escape racism and politics, and baseball cards are no different. If you had to ask a typical, competent dealer for a single piece of advice on investing in cards, he would say, "Buy white, and buy New York." This statement reveals a remarkably provincial, reactionary, and elitist point of view, but it is unfortunately sound thinking. Nobody wants it to be this way, but we live in an unjust world. Some people in the business hope that dealers will begin pushing the cards of black stars more fervently than those of whites. But this is perhaps placing too much responsibility and pressure on them. The buyers, not the sellers, ultimately make the market in collectibles. I don't know a single dealer who wouldn't rather get $15 or $20 for a Stewart rookie card than $6.

One other corollary to the black versus white theory comes from the fact that baseball, invented in 1839, was played exclusively by whites until 1945. Nonwhites have been in the majors for less than 50 years, so they were deprived of producing stars in the ancient era of the game. It took the editors of Macmillan's *Baseball Encyclopedia* eight editions to finally compile enough data about the Negro leagues to include some of those stats in that tome. The latest edition lists scant, incomplete statistics, but at least there is some recognition.

The market in white baseball stars is higher and moves up faster than that of comparable—or even better—players who are black or from the Dominican Republic. (Of current star player prices Jose Canseco may be an exception. He was born in Cuba, and despite his controversial statements about racism in baseball's awards voting, most fans view him as wholly American.)

Let's take the most striking examples: Mickey Mantle, Willie Mays, and Hank Aaron. They are probably the three most revered and remembered baseball stars of the 1950s and 1960s, and their cards are coveted and known by even the most casual collectors. Yet Mantle's 1952 Topps card is worth six or seven times more than Mays' card, despite the fact that they are equally difficult to find. Only Aaron's 1954 Topps rookie card exceeds four figures.

If you had to rate the three players by ability, most baseball historians and experts would rank them Aaron, Mays, Mantle (or Mays, Aaron, Mantle), in descending order. Nobody who is knowledgeable thinks Mantle was a better player than the other two except Bill James, who claims in his *Historical Abstract* book that Mantle had better "peak" career years than Mays. And that might be true, but peak years do not make a whole career.

Mantle was the master of the towering home run, the clutch hit, and a World Series star because he was lucky enough to play on a team that was constantly competing in the Fall Classic. Mays, naturally, was a tremendous home run hitter and one of the greatest defensive center fielders who ever played. He was probably the most exciting of the three players. And even your grandmother knows Aaron broke Ruth's home run record. It's not worth poring over their statistics and arguing about them, because true fans who have seen all three play the game know their talents differed ever so slightly and went far beyond the box scores.

But let's consider the factors that affect the price of their cards: their playing venues and their personalities. Hammerin' Henry Aaron played in Milwaukee and Atlanta, which hardly draw the media attention that is apparent in a bigger market like New York, where Mantle played his entire career. Willie Mays played first in New York and then the bulk of his career in San Francisco. Nothing wrong with San Francisco, but it's not the same as the Big Apple when it comes to national press attention. The Mick was the man who played nearly every home game in the same spot Joe DiMaggio did in the House that Ruth Built.

Of the three players, their personalities are possibly more alike than we might ever know, but that is not the way they were portrayed by sportswriters for two decades. Aaron was always low-key, unassuming, and fairly reserved. A lovely guy, but not that interesting. From the Madison Avenue viewpoint, lovely doesn't sell as well as wholesome, brash, or even macho. Mays, the Say Hey Kid, always came to the park with the agility of a cat and a smile to match it, but he was never very articulate (few good ball players are) or particularly outgoing. In fact, he has a notoriously gruff reputation when he signs autographs at card shows.

Mantle is a special case because he carried on his shoulders—figuratively, at least—the most successful sports franchise in the nation's history. (The Yankees franchise may have reached its nadir in 1990 when Steinbrenner was forced to divest himself from day-to-day operation of the team, but it did not hurt the club's market value per se. In fact, Commissioner Fay Vincent's action may have enhanced it. The Yankees are still valued at between $200 million and $350 million.) A good-looking, muscular, country boy from Oklahoma, Mantle epitomized what America wanted in a baseball hero: a great white slugger. Middle-aged mothers and fathers who never went to a ball game other than their kids' Little League games know who Mickey Mantle is, even if they can't recall any specific feats. Mantle hit home runs, and he hit them frequently, especially in the World Series, and perhaps most important, he hit them very far. The collector apparently does not care to remind himself that both Mays and Aaron hit more.

The above treatise does not mean I think that Mays and Aaron cards are bad buys. On the contrary, they're very good (and you'll notice, very expensive), because these cards may have more potential in the 1990s than Mantle's cards.

MR. MINT'S MAXIM: *Long distance always sells better than batting average. Home run hitters also are better buys than power pitchers. In fact, even great singles hitters' baseball cards (Rose, Carew, Cobb, to name perhaps the three best known) increase at a faster rate than almost every great pitcher*

(Cy Young, Christy Mathewson, Walter Johnson, Tom Seaver, and Nolan Ryan are the five most notable exceptions).

The complexion of the card and collectible buyer reflects the complexion of the market. The great majority of collectors in this country are white and middle-class or just plain very affluent. They are men and boys, few women and girls. There are very few blacks who collect cards, and the number of other minorities is quite small. I rarely see any foreigners at card shows; more likely they're Asian-Americans who are 14-year-old dealers when they're not working on their science projects. Only recently have the Japanese become large collectors and investors, because the numbers are now becoming seriously large. Maybe not van Gogh and Cézanne big, but still fairly attractive. And everyone knows the Japanese have a lot of money to invest in the United States. But these high rollers aren't parading through shows shopping for rookie cards. They're discreetly buying large old collections, mainly through auctions and dealers on the West Coast. They're buying Ruth, Gehrig, Wagner, and Cobb; they're scoffing up tobacco cards and Goudey cards from the 1930s. They're buying the equivalent of blue chips stocks, and not much else.

There are, of course, exceptions to every trend, and there are some notable black players whose card prices remain strong and still have a very high potential upside. Along with Mays and Aaron, they are Roy Campanella, Jackie Robinson, Satchel Paige, Roberto Clemente, and Reggie Jackson. All are Hall of Famers except for Reggie Jackson, who is a virtual certainty to be elected in his first year of eligibility (1992).

But each player was special in his own way.

Campanella was the great catcher and mainstay of the Brooklyn Dodgers until his career was cut short by a tragic auto accident. The feisty, base-running Robinson, of course, broke baseball's color line.

The famous T-206 Honus Wagner Piedmont Tobacco card (1909–1911) is considered the most coveted card in the business. This one had a slight crease in the collar but it's still worth $50,000 or more in any condition.

Mickey Mantle's Topps 1952 card is the most expensive postwar baseball card. This one is in near mint to mint condition and is valued at $7,500. Had the card been perfectly centered it would be worth $12,000 or more.

Reggie Jackson's Topps rookie card from the 1969 series is difficult to find in top condition. This is about as good as the centering gets. Near mint or better cards are $400 to $600, and sometimes more. The price of this card will probably increase dramatically when Jackson is inducted in the Hall of Fame.

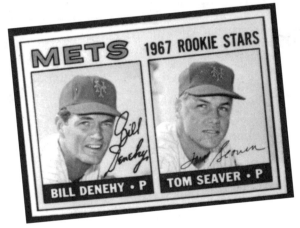

Bill Denehy's claim to baseball fame is that he appears with the legendary Tom Seaver on the 1967 Topps rookie card. It's not unusual for a great specimen to bring $1,500 to $2,000.

Yaz's 1960 Topps rookie card books for approximately $350 in near mint to mint condition. They sell well in Boston.

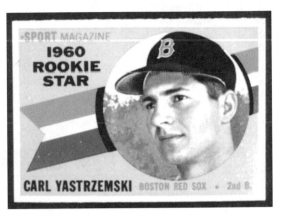

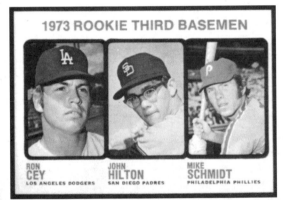

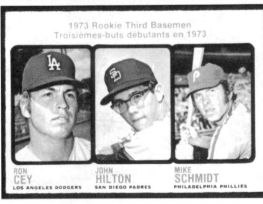

These two rookie cards of Philly's Hall of Fame-bound third baseman illustrate an important and often misunderstood quirk in the marketplace. The O-P-C is the Canadian issue and much scarcer than the American counterpart (although they're virtually the same card). But because demand is lower for Canadian cards, the American version books for nearly triple the value ($325 versus $125).

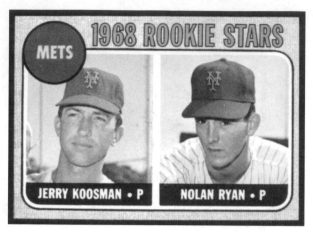

The very expensive ($1,200 to $1,500) Nolan Ryan rookie card from the 1968 Topps series. Only sainthood could make the demand for this card any greater, and I feel it's vastly overvalued considering how easy it is to find one in mint condition.

This 1933 Goudey Babe Ruth card was double printed in that series, but it still holds a value of $3,000 or more in near mint condition. This one is as nice as you'll find, despite the slight stain marring the upper-left-hand corner. I can never be too bullish on investing in the Babe.

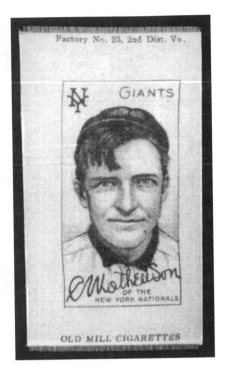

Two of the greatest pitchers of all time appeared on the very desirable "silk" sets issued around 1911 by Old Mill cigarettes.

A Babe Ruth single-signed ball is not difficult to find, but it always brings $3,000 to $5,000 depending on whether the signature is sharp and the ball hasn't yellowed.

Collecting old jerseys of stars, such as this 1972 sleeveless Pirates shirt worn by Roberto Clemente, is a solid investment. Beware of the newer nylon jerseys because they're often sold as "game worn" when they've never seen the inside of a ball park.

Brooklyn Dodger great Gil Hodges' Rawlings first baseman's mitt has everything a careful collector would want: quality condition, a Hall of Fame name, and absolute scarcity. This is the type of item a serious investor should always look to buy.

Joe Cronin's bat, glove, and home jersey from the Red Sox 1946 season are the kinds of items that interest top collectors, not to mention the curators from the Hall of Fame collection in Cooperstown.

This baseball is a lesson in what not to do. The ball was signed on the sweet spot by Jackie Robinson and Ted Williams. It's worth only a few hundred dollars because Williams' signature devalued it greatly. It would have been worth at least $2,500 with Robinson's signature by itself.

World Series scorecards and programs are among the most-sought-after collectibles in the hobby. Red Sox appearances, as every fan knows, are rare, so these old programs are especially good investments. Condition is critical for top value; worn spines and tears in the covers greatly decrease their value.

Official Score Card
New York Giants vs. Boston Red Sox
Champions of the National League / Champions of the American League
At the BRUSH STADIUM
WORLD'S CHAMPIONSHIP SERIES · 1912 ·
Price 10 Cents

CHAMPIONS 1912
RED SOX
WORLD'S SERIES
FENWAY PARK · BOSTON ·
Souvenir Biography & Score Book
Price, 10 Cents

Official Score Card
1930
Price 25¢
For the Championship of the World
St. Louis vs Philadelphia

This 1933 All-Star game ball is signed on the sweet spot by Lou Gehrig and Lefty Grove, both rare autographs. What makes it so highly desirable is the top quality condition of the signatures and the ball.

Eddie Collins, the great Hall of Fame second baseman, signed this beautiful ball, albeit not on the sweet spot. Since his single-signed balls are so rare, the placement of the autograph isn't that critical. This kind of item (at $2,000 to $3,000) will always be in demand.

A New York Yankees press pin from the 1956 World Series is worth about $300. The Dodger version from that year is considerably rarer, and it brings about $2,500.

This 1919 World Series ticket stub has special meaning because the White Sox apparently threw this game to the Reds in the most infamous scandal in baseball history.

Babe Ruth might have been the most merchandised ball player in history. His endorsements and appearances were so numerous they are impossible to catalogue completely. Even a pocket watch, wristwatch, and a scorer from his early years in Boston are nice collectibles.

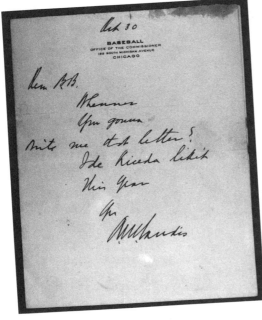

This letter signed by Judge Kenesaw Mountain Landis, the first commissioner of baseball, is the type of autograph avid collectors want to add to their caches.

If you're going to invest in autographed photos, stick to the old black-and-white ones such as this rare shot of Connie Mack outside a batting cage. What makes this even nicer is his inscription to Frankie Frisch.

Unopened wax packs of baseball cards have enjoyed a vogue among collectors and investors in the past few years. This one retailed for a nickel in 1952. In early 1990 it was still a relative bargain at $600. By the end of that year these packs were in demand at $1,500 to $1,900 apiece. Even the wrappers bring a few hundred dollars.

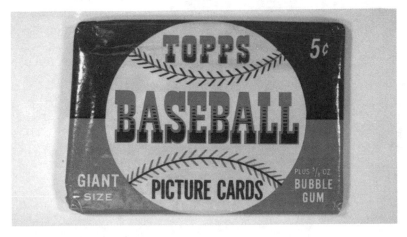

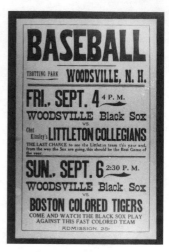

Negro leagues memorabilia—a poster and ticket to the 1947 Negro World Series at the Polo Grounds—are increasingly difficult to find and have recently piqued the interest of historians and baseball scholars. Accordingly, collecting interest has also soared.

The 1936 All-Star game program (hosted by the Boston Braves) is a very tough item to find. I've seen very few, especially in such beautiful condition. On items like these I'll pay more and then offer them to my top clients first.

Jackie Robinson appeared on Bowman cards between 1949 and 1951, but his 1952 and 1953 Topps cards are nicer looking and worth more money. This beautiful 1953 issue shows how the gloss and brightness can be retained even after almost four decades.

This E-102 Ty Cobb card was issued circa 1910. I especially like it because it's an innocent, boyish pose of the fiery Tiger ball player who was one of the best to play the game, despite his controversial reputation.

Few people remember Mickey Mantle's "Grand Slam" baseball game, but when this example surfaced a collector paid $650 for it.

The American League All-Star pennant from 1958 is the kind of item that everyone remembers from his youth. Unfortunately, few survive in perfect shape because kids (myself included) tacked them all over their bedroom walls.

Paige pitched for most of his career in the Negro leagues. He didn't make the majors until he was 42 years old, and he had a losing record in six seasons. But collectors and fans remember his colorful pitching motion, vibrant personality, and his witty if fractured sayings. (Can you imagine having Yogi Berra and Satchel Paige together for dinner? What a comedy act.)

Clemente was a brilliant ball player who in 18 seasons hit less than .300 only once, and had exactly 3,000 hits before his untimely death. Killed in a plane that crashed while on the way to aid Nicaraguan earthquake victims, Clemente was the first great Puerto Rican superstar.

MR. MINT'S MAXIM: *Reggie Jackson is the most significant example of the black ball players' baseball cards whose price is on a constant rise. Jax transcends the color line. I predict his rookie card, the 1969 Topps, will easily top $1,000 in near mint to mint condition by the time he's inducted at Cooperstown.*

I came to this conclusion only after carefully considering all the factors, both the card itself and the other factors that make Jackson different from the conventional black superstar. First, the card. It is in the second series, which for some reason had a lower print run than all the others but the high series. The commons in that series are worth about the same as those in the high-numbered series. The Jackson card is what's known as a tough card; there aren't that many around, especially in premium shape. Next, the best centering on the card is commonly 60–40. Only very rarely do you see a perfectly centered portrait.

Then there's Reggie Jackson the man and the player. His

venue couldn't have made him more media-visible. He's played in Oakland, Anaheim, and New York, but his personality fully bloomed when he was a Yankee. He had a perfect blend of arrogance when he worked for Steinbrenner and Billy Martin. His inimical look when he admired his round-trippers was as memorable as Ruth's home run trot. He was brilliant in the clutch, including those three home runs he hit in a single World Series game. Mr. October even had a touch of humility, saying that for one night he might consider himself a true superstar. A minority remembers, but nobody cares, that Reggie is at the top of the all-time strikeout list.

As a retired ball player, Jackson has stayed active in the game and participated in card shows. Unlike Darryl Strawberry, he actually signs his name so collectors can read it. He is a baseball card collector himself, and among the many rumors circulating in the business is his desire to sell his own autographed rookie cards. He has been hoarding #260, paying top dollar ($450 and up), apparently until he has at least 563, which corresponds to his career home run total. Then he plans to market them as a signed, numbered, limited edition after he's inducted into the Hall of Fame. What will he ask for those cards? Probably $1,000 or more (which gives him a potential gross profit of $250,000). What about the fact that collectors don't like baseball cards with autographs? Is he special enough for this scheme to work? Well, I can't answer that. But I do know this: Whether it works or not, the price of Jackson cards will continue to increase dramatically. It is at the top of my list of recommended buys in single cards.

In addition to ethnicity and personality, there is a critical factor that collectors often overlook, and that is power hitters versus singles hitters. Jose Canseco puts it best, as he did in a 1990 *Sports Illustrated* interview:

> Which would you rather see, a guy who goes three for three in a game with no RBIs or a guy who doesn't get a hit all night until he hits a three-run homer to win the game? Would you rather see Wade Boggs get two

hits the opposite way or me hit a 500-foot home run?

People even enjoy watching me strike out, because I swing so hard. That's where the excitement is. It's the whole Roger Clemens confrontation. The 98-miles-per-hour fastball going against me. I might strike out four times but my oh for four is more exciting than Wade Boggs getting two hits the opposite way.

I've got to agree with Canseco, and that's how it is when it comes to cards. Nobody yet knows whether he'll end up with as many dingers as Mantle, but he's certainly pressing the pace. In his first five seasons, he hit 160, whereas Mantle had only 121. He hit more in his first five seasons than Hank Aaron (but less than Mays, Ruth, and Reggie Jackson). And Canseco only had 17 in 1989, when he missed half the season with an injury. Yes, the guy can park a lot of those Rawlings. If booming home runs, and lots of them, are still the major Hall of Fame yardstick in 10 years, and assuming Canseco is still hitting them, then he certainly will be considered a serious candidate for the Hall.

Is it too premature to compare Canseco with Mantle and the other home run greats? Of course. But there's no harm in projecting and conjecturing, which is one reason why Canseco cards are already overvalued. Dealers and collectors follow the statistics as closely as anyone.

So, bottom line, are whoppingly expensive Mickey Mantle baseball cards still a good investment? At this point, I don't think Mantle cards will ever drop in price—not any of the 40-odd Bowman and Topps cards ever made. But I do think the peak *rate* of increase has been reached, and the market for the next few years might be viewed as soft. In 1990, a gem mint 1952 Topps card was being offered for sale at $13,000 by a New York dealer. His ad claimed that the most important postwar card (true) would be the first to top $25,000. Yes, it has the best chance of that, but when? I do not think it's going to double in a year or even two or three years. (As this book went to the printer, Sotheby's auction gallery was gearing up for a major baseball card and collectible sale where the presale estimate on a gem mint 1952 Mantle card—from my find—was $10,000 to $15,000.)

MR. MINT'S MAXIM: *You cannot lose money buying a famous Hall of Fame player's baseball card, because he cannot strike out anymore, nor can he lose any more games. Note the qualifying word "famous." There are, for example, Hall of Famers like Bobby Doerr, Ralph Kiner, Luis Aparicio, and Monte Irvin whose cards are low or modestly priced who will always have limited appeal, and thus limited profit potential.*

There are some other soft spots in the card market of famous players, and they include Ruth, Gehrig, and Cobb in anything less than near mint condition. You already know that I don't advise buying any cards in off condition at all, but I'm just trying to deliver you from temptation among the earliest, best-known stars. You will see many, many ads talking about "affordable greats" or "reasonably priced deceased Hall of Fame player" cards in very good to excellent condition. They're the epitome of the stagnant market. Many are around, they're all for sale, and nobody is buying them.

There are still undervalued star and rookie cards, and they include Ted Williams, Sandy Koufax, Stan Musial, and Harmon Killebrew. These cards are far better investments than Mantle cards, because they have an upside potential of four or five times that of Mantle cards. Even though they'll never achieve the same value as Mantle cards, my feeling is that they'll eventually catch up percentagewise in terms of growth.

Consider how the Hall of Fame (or HOF, as it's known in the card trade) hypes the price of a card, especially when it's compared with a player of equal stature and ability. One of the best examples is that of two highly regarded shortstops, Pee Wee Reese and Phil Rizzuto. Reese is in the Hall, and Rizzuto is not. You need not bother comparing their careers; trust me, they're uncannily equal. Reese played in Brooklyn for some very famous teams, and Rizzuto, of course, looked over his shoulder at DiMag in the outfield grass. Should Reese's card be 2½ times the value of Rizzuto's? Probably not. But the 1953 Bowman Reese #33 booked for $225 to $250, while the Bowman Rizzuto #9 sold for $90 to $100. (Had Reese not made the HOF, and had either of those guys played for any franchise other than Brooklyn and New York, their cards would be little better than commons.)

The HOF factor influences a player's card value in concrete yet subtle ways as a ball player with any chance of election approaches the twilight years of his career. Mike Schmidt's rookie card, a high-numbered series from Topps 1973 issue, will rise slightly as he approaches certain election to the Hall. Since his first-ballot election is indisputable, the card's price has already had the greatest amount of inflation. When Joe Morgan was elected in 1990, his 1965 rookie card immediately jumped in price, even though it's in the first and easiest series. It has likely seen its biggest growth. Steve Carlton's rookie card comes from the same set and it's in the midseries. It will probably take one nice price jump when Carlton is elected to the HOF, but collectors are already buying Carlton cards because he is a first-ballot sure thing. Carlton is selling for $400 plus and his card will most certainly be going for $750 to $800 in 1993.

Nolan Ryan, the man with the mechanical arm, is a singular example of a rookie card that is, in my judgment, grossly overvalued. Last season, his sixth no-hitter and his 300-win game seemed to juice the price a little more of the 1968 Topps "Mets Rookies" Jerry Koosman/Nolan Ryan card #177. Book value, according to Beckett's was $950, and it was trading at 130 to 170 percent of that price. Every show I attended had Ryan cards for sale at $1,200 to $1,500 in prime condition. Occasionally, you'd see a fabulous-looking one for sale at $1,700 or $1,800. Even if he pitches until he's 50 years old, and gets another no-hitter, the market has already accounted for his greatness, the 5,000 strikeouts, and all his deeds, and dead-solid admission to the HOF.

As a dealer, it was interesting to see the vast number of Ryan rookie cards for sale in 1990. It was as if they'd just come out of the woodwork. Even low-volume weekend guys with nothing but $60 and $70 cards in off condition in their showcases happen to have a near mint or better Ryan. Why? Well, they'd all bought them in the previous two years for $350 to $400 and were attempting to take advantage of what they obviously believed to be peak market. I can't blame them, but I couldn't recommend a strong buy order to investors who look to me for advice.

If you're insistent on buying a Nolan Ryan card, his second year 1969 Topps #533 is probably a better investment. It's a fourth-series card and is actually scarcer than the 1968 rookie. It can be bought for 20 to 30 percent of the price of the rookie, too.

Hall of Fame potential from rookie cards from the 1960s has pretty much been exhausted. The guys who are going to get in have already been elected. The borderline retired players are Don Sutton, and Tommy John. John, who won 288 games and was a three-time 20-game winner, wouldn't, in my opinion, even fetch the $50 to $60 asking price for his 1964 rookie card had he not played with the Yankees at the end of his career. Sutton won 300 games and has that personable California smile, but he won 20 games only once. Remember, the two possibles from the 1960s are pitchers, and therefore have less potential than hitters. The sportswriters who vote for HOFers are sometimes obstinate, flaky, and unpredictable (just like card collectors).

Three hundred wins, 3,000 hits, and 500 home runs are supposed to be certain benchmarks for admission to the Hall, but nobody knows for sure how writers feel when they fill out the ballots.

Players who began their career in the 1970s will surely produce HOFers, but who are they? Yes, it's a lot more difficult to tell, though some players are throwing up some very nice numbers and will be seriously considered when they're retired for five years—probably the late 1990s, or maybe not until after the year 2000. George Brett, Robin Yount, Carlton Fisk, and Dave Winfield are the four players who immediately come to mind, as well as pitcher Bert Blyleven. I would put Yount at a 75 percent chance of election to the Hall, and Brett at about the same. Fisk should probably make it because of his longevity and career stats as a catcher, but that doesn't mean that all voters see it the way I do. I'd put him at an 80 percent chance. (Bob Boone, the only other active catcher, I put at 40 to 50 percent chance.)

Winfield is about 30 to 50 percent possible based on his career (and also because sportswriters always favored him in his long-term disputes with Steinbrenner). Steve Garvey, Dale Murphy, Gary Carter, Jim Rice, and Eddie Murray all have a shot, but I'd rate them all somewhere between faint chance and possible, or about 25 to 40 percent, depending on the player.

MR. MINT'S MAXIM: *Of the 1980s cards, Rickey Henderson's rookie card is probably the most desired (yes, it still books for more than Canseco's 1986 Donruss and Mattingly's 1984 Donruss). He has a minimum 90 percent chance (a conservative viewpoint; many dealers feel he's an absolute 100 percent certainty) to be elected to the HOF. But his card is readily available in mint condition in large quantities. He's a good investment, but you may have to hold it for several years until it reaches the high three-figure mark.*

After race, player position, and power versus average, the single factor most often overlooked in the price of baseball cards is the local market. Regionalism, as well as racism, helps define why some classes of cards are worth more than others. The collectors with the most money, and therefore the greatest influence on the overall market, live in the big cities: New York, Los Angeles, Chicago, Boston, Philadelphia, and the San Francisco–Oakland area. The equivalent card will likely cost more in any urban area than it will in a tiny suburb of a state with a smaller population.

It pays to buy Phillies players at New York card shows and sell them in Philadelphia. Conversely, you'd want to buy Mets stars in Atlanta and sell them in New York.

MR. MINT'S MAXIM: *Any baseball card or collectible item is worth more in the player's home city than it will be in some other locale.*

Pete Rose costs more in Cincinnati than he does in New York, but you'll pay more for Darryl Strawberry in Queens than you will in Oakland, where Canseco and Rickey Henderson cost more than New York collectors might deem reasonable. The bull market of Ernie Banks cards is in Chicago. You probably can't get the highest price for a gem Al Kaline card unless you're calling dealers in Detroit.

You're obviously wondering what I think of the potential of Pete Rose's Topps 1963 rookie card. I wanted to save my analysis of Rose for the end of this chapter, because the player and the man are apparently so different. On the field, Charlie Hustle's career was par excellence, the all-time leading hitter. Based on player merit alone, he is a HOFer. But he's certainly had a checkered career off the field; while many players have undoubtedly commingled with gamblers and bet on games, no player has done jail time for failing to report income from the sale of his memorabilia and personal items. Rose has undoubtedly broken new ground as far as controversy goes. In straw polls, sportswriters appear to be fairly evenly split on whether they're going to vote for his HOF election in his first year of eligibility. (There is a "character" clause in the requirement guidelines, so those writers who loved him—yet feel he somehow betrayed the image of the game—are not so sure whether they'll include him on their ballots.)

MR. MINT'S MAXIM: *Whether Pete Rose is elected to the HOF should not appreciably affect the very strong demand of his cards, especially his rookie card.*

Only two things can happen:

If he's elected to the HOF, the price of Pete Rose cards will go up further.

If he's not, they will still increase.

The controversy over his gambling problem is either immaterial or has made his card more desirable. The American public is fickle but forgiving. The fact that Rose epitomized the game for 24 years will overshadow his indiscretions. I'm still bullish on Pete, and so are collectors. (As we went to press, the rule makers at Cooperstown apparently amended the requirements to exclude Rose's name from sportswriters ballots. To some observers the issue is closed. Pete Rose will not get in the Hall of Fame. But there's always a chance he'll be forgiven and elected some time in the future.)

COLLECTING MEMORABILIA, PART 1: A TOUR OF TODAY'S AUTOGRAPH FACTORIES

One of the hottest areas for collectors and investors is the market in old items of baseball nostalgia, especially those with autographs. I predict noncard objets d'art will experience healthy growth in the 1990s, perhaps even at the level that some cards achieved in the 1980s.

There are two reasons. First, many new investors with a lot of cash are coming into the business and they don't want to bother with the effort it takes to learn about cards. Second, other investors who already own cards have exhausted their interest in them and are looking to diversify their portfolios. They are attracted to artifacts because they have more of a mystique, less is known about their market value, and after a few months or even a year, everyone thinks the investor is an expert.

Some cynicism about cards is undoubtedly juicing the collectibles market. Old-time baseball card collectors, the pioneers of the hobby, are disillusioned by what they think are unrealistically high prices on cards and are looking for something else with investment potential.

There are perhaps better buys in the noncard part of baseball collectibles, mainly because there are few, if any, reliable price guides. Only the most diligent and industrious collectors and dealers know what these items are truly worth. Beckett has published two recent annual price guides to baseball collectibles, and although the contents lists well over 100 different items, the emphasis is on sets of coins, discs, cereal packages, pins, stickers, and stamps. Most of these things are low-priced, and if you begin by putting some money here, I advise you to stick to investing in complete collections rather than individual pieces, mainly because you'll be wasting a lot of time on very small deals.

The 1963 Salada tea metal coins, for example, book for more than $625 in near mint condition for the entire 63-player run. But the Mantle, Aaron, and Mays are worth a third of the total. Why buy a $20 Eddie Mathews coin and hope the price doubles in six months? If it does, sure, you made a good call, but you'll net only $20, and you spend more than that in gas when you go to a card show. Also, most of these items, while legitimate collectibles, are too obscure to easily dispose of; you will have trouble finding buyers. Trust me; there is a very low demand for the likes of 1964 Detroit Tiger lids (except possibly in the Motor City) or 1982 Drake's cards.

When you begin exploring the market for high-demand, higher-priced antiques, you are venturing into uncharted territory. Of the most popular items in today's collectibles market—balls, bats, jerseys, pennants, Hall of Fame postcards or plaques, original advertising posters, point-of-purchase displays, and press pins—Beckett's guide lists prices on only three items: all the press pins from the World Series, All-Star games, and Hall of Fame annual induction ceremonies.

But don't groan about that lack of available price guide information all that much. Remember, most of the other wanderers onto this terrain don't have a road map either. Much of my own pricing on these goods is pure educated guesswork based mostly on experience: What is a fair price? Or what will the market reasonably bear for quick sale? When someone asks how I arrived at a given figure, I often use the recent selling price of an item comparable in rarity, condition, and demand. If I see an autographed baseball with eight HOF signatures—none very famous—I might put each autograph at $20 to $25 (or whatever the current market value is) and offer $175 for the ball.

For example, take a Pete Rose autograph on a Tampa dog track program. The program itself is not particularly interesting, nor is Rose's signature very difficult to find. But this item has a deeper implication because of his gambling exploits. The market on Pete Rose remains strong, despite (or because) of his tumultuous personal life, and I knew a Rose collector would want something that is slightly different or unusual. This is an example of that. Since his signature on an autographed ball is common, and regularly sells for only $25 or $35, I figured the price of his autograph on a race track program—how many baseball fans could he have signed for that day?—was at least 10 times as rare. I sold the program for $250. Was it a good investment? I know a collector who said he would have paid $750 for it right after I sold it. Even if he's stretching it, the program was certainly a better investment than taking a chance on 10 Pete Rose signed balls.

Obviously, you must do a substantial amount of homework before you plunk down $1,000 for an autographed Mickey Mantle bat or $3,500 for a George Sisler signed baseball. You should even be fluent with the market on items in the three-figure range before you make an initial investment.

Before you do anything, acquaint yourself with the substantial distinction between a true antique or piece of memorabilia and a "current collectible." There are no hard rules here, because things that are "collected" are not antiques until they mature and become old. Some of these things may increase in value immediately, however. And though every antique is a collectible, not every antique is worth a lot of money or is a good investment. In 1990, Christie's auction house sold a pair of Max Carey's cleats for only $350, half the presale estimate. Do not feel ignorant about Max Carey. Only ardent fans and old-timers know who Carey was. (He played for Pittsburgh in the teens and 1920s, and he got into the Hall of Fame because he stole 738 bases and hit .285.)

True relics tend to be items of genuine nostalgia but also of very well known or famous players, such as an Eddie Collins glove or a jersey worn by Brooks Robinson. Or Lefty Grove's Boston Red Sox warm-up jacket, or a Ty Cobb game-used bat. How much should you pay for Lou Gehrig's uniform from Columbia University? What would you lay out for Gehrig's high school yearbook in fairly worn condition?

On the other hand, some signed items gain value very quickly because of the quirky demands of collectors. Many years ago, Barry Halper, the limited partner of the New York Yankees, and the collector with the most voracious appetite outside of Cooperstown, happened to be in the clubhouse when Reggie Jackson was about to discard a worn-out batting glove. Halper told Reggie he ought to keep it, sign it, and donate it to a charity auction. Jackson did, and the item fetched $250. Though it has nowhere near the history of Max Carey's cleats, it was probably a better buy.

There are current collectibles, too, that refer to recently manufactured merchandise, like a statue of Jose Canseco or Don Mattingly, certainly genuine items, but they cost far less money, and they are usually of dubious collectible value.

MR. MINT'S MAXIM: *Avoid anything that even remotely smells like gimmick merchandise. Just because a player, his estate, or major-league baseball licenses an item doesn't make it necessarily valuable or desirable.*

Forgive my crankiness here, but I cannot imagine anyone who would want a Bobbin' Head doll of Babe Ruth that was newly manufactured in an edition of 5,000. The doll's head looks nothing at all like Ruth, yet the merchandise has been licensed by the Babe's estate. The retail price is only $34.95.

Think a bit about the math when you see these kinds of ads. If the edition sells out, the company grosses nearly $175,000. It probably paid a modest advance against royalties to the Ruth estate, and the manufacturing cost of the doll couldn't be more than a few dollars apiece. Subtracting overhead (like advertising, postage, the distributor's cut), the company stands to clear quite a nifty profit if it sells out, and it takes little up-front cash risk if the doll is a total bomb.

Is this a desirable collectible? Not for me. Not for you, either.

While the company makes no claims as to future resale value, what do you think it will be worth in 1992? Or in 20 years? If you buy this object, you are putting your money and trust not in the single object, but in the success or failure of the entire enterprise. If the company sells only a hundred of these dolls, the only way they'll ever be worth any money (years from when you bought it) is if the unsold dolls are destroyed and very few others besides yours survive.

I've noticed recently that some doll ads on television carry disclaimers saying that buyers cannot automatically assume that they will increase in price. Think of the brilliant psychology here. Not only does the marketer cover himself legally, but he ever so subtly puts the suggestion in the viewer's mind that the doll just might be a "collectible" item in the future. By promising nothing, the ad has carefully dropped the hint that you might be passing up the buy of a lifetime.

Another example. There was a full-page ad in SCD informing the sports hobbyist of the availability of "gold edition collector plates." These 10¼-inch-diameter plates with 23K-gold borders with the player's signature (facsimile) fixed permanently on the plate cost only $150 for either Tom Seaver, Sam Musial, or a Snider, Mantle, and Mays combo. Or you can buy Gregg Jeffries for a discount at $125. Or, if the price was too stiff, you could buy a 4¼-inch-diameter mini-plate of any of the above for just $19.95. The plates come with letters of authenticity (as if anyone would want to copy them), and each plate was produced in a limited edition (ranging from 1,900 to 3,500), except for Jeffries, whose edition was unspecified. (I guess Gregg is too young to be in a limited edition.)

In the same issue of SCD, you could buy a 10-inch-high Don Mattingly figurine in his batting stance for only $295 (or, if you prefer, Will Clark, Mark McGwire, Bo Jackson, or Nolan Ryan). I can't imagine anyone reselling these things for any kind of profit sometime soon after they're purchased. This should seem rather pedestrian advice to all but the uninitiated, but every day I am newly surprised by some marginal (I'm being polite here) piece of baseball merchandise people are willing to pay $100 or $200 for.

MR. MINT'S MAXIM: *Current memorabilia (if you'll excuse the oxymoron) autographed by living superstars or Hall of Fame players have a legitimate collectible and investment value (albeit modest), because these players regularly appear at shows and there is a fair market price for their signatures.*

Nobody is absolutely certain whether promoter, dealer, or player dreamed up the idea of charging money for an autograph, but it is safe to assume that it had its origins in baseball. Some claim it was Bob Feller who began asking $5 to sign, because the former Cleveland HOF pitcher felt he was entitled to or needed the money, or some combination thereof. If this is true, then Feller probably had no inkling as to the massive industry he was helping to create. Currently, the three top-earning signers on a per-show basis are Jose Canseco ($50,000), Joe DiMaggio ($45,000), and Mickey Mantle ($40,000).

For instance, the market value of Mickey Mantle's autograph has been steadily increasing every year. (You can actually get Mantle to sign for free, if you happen to catch him in a conducive mood at the restaurant which bears his name on Central Park South in New York City. But he won't autograph a bat. I'll explain why later.) In the mid-1980s, Mantle would sign at shows for $10 or $15, and the price he charged promoters steadily increased (to the point where he gets as much for an afternoon's work as he once did for playing ball for an entire season). A Mantle autograph is worth about $35 on his 8" by 10" glossy, $40 to $50 on an official American League ball.

MR. MINT'S MAXIM: *It doesn't necessarily matter if an item is newly manufactured or has aged for 20 years or more in a trunk in somebody's attic. The key to its worth is whether it belonged to a famous player and/or has his autograph. The older the item, and the older the signature, the higher it will be appraised.*

Common sense should dictate that Phil Rizzuto's signature in blue felt-tip pen on a Yankees publicity photo showing the Scooter as an announcer from the 1980s will be worth somewhat less to a serious collector than an old publicity glossy of a young Rizzuto in uniform that was signed with a fountain or ballpoint pen in the 1940s or 1950s (assuming the old picture is not yellowed or damaged). The former is a newly minted collectible; the latter is an antique. A Yankees collector might pay only $10 or $15 for the new picture but at least $20, and possibly as much as $30 to $50, for the old one.

The other obvious point is that dead men can't sign autographs.

The market in any baseball item with a deceased HOF player is stronger and higher than those of living HOF players. I don't want to sound ghoulish about discussing some of the older baseball greats (most of whom will sign for very little money), but the reality is that they're not going to be alive forever. Actually, even the most hard-hearted dealers hope they'll sign until they're 100 years old—especially the cooperative players who are courteous to collectors, don't cancel show appearances, and arrive promptly.

Of all the living HOFers 14 are in their 70s, seven are in their 80s, and three (umpire Al Barlick, former commissioner Happy Chandler, and Joe Sewell) are in their 90s. Signatures from living HOFers (and those who died recently) are quite plentiful, because they've been signing at shows for several years now. Their autograph prices are fairly stable. Do not expect any price increases until they stop signing.

Bill Dickey, Cool Papa Bell, Charlie Gehringer, and Al Lopez do not sign much anymore because of infirmity or old age, so their signatures are in slightly greater demand and already cost roughly double what other living HOFers sell for. Roy Campanella, as most collectors already know, has been disabled for many years, and can sign autographs only with the assistance of a glove-type device that holds his pen. (It does not enable him to sign anything but a flat item.) Anything with Campy's name on it, naturally, is a blue chip item, but items signed prior to his January 1958 accident are rare and worth much more than those autographed with the device.

MR. MINT'S MAXIM: *Demand is the key to collecting the signatures of living HOFers. The autographs of some current superstars can cost as much as a HOFer who regularly appears and signs at shows. Johnny Bench, the youngest member of the HOF, signs so much that mail requests for autographs often resulted* *in his sending out rubber-stamp facsimiles. (He is neither the first nor the only player to mass-produce his autograph.)*

For example, Robin Yount's autograph is in fairly strong demand, especially among midwestern fans. Though Yount will sign at ballparks when it's convenient, he doesn't like to sign at shows. (And no fan could blame him. He's one of the highest-paid players.) So his autographed baseball costs about $30 or $35, while Warren Spahn signed balls cost only $15 or $18. Spahn, of course, is number five on the all-time win list for pitchers, while Yount is not yet retired. Like or not, Yount's autograph is double that of Spahn's and also many other HOFers who never earned as much money in a season as Yount does in a week. Again, Canseco's autograph is relatively expensive at $35 to $40 (and plentiful), because Oakland kids and other collectors have great faith in his future. And Canseco has been known to rarely refuse a free request, even when he's in a lousy mood.

Nolan Ryan, again, is a special case, and his autographed baseballs hover at the $35 to $40 mark. His signed, numbered, limited edition (5,000, for the number of strikeouts) costs double, and that's probably not a bad investment. It's the same signed ball, but Ryan might have signed 50,000 or 100,000 other balls already, so it's rarer.

MR. MINT'S MAXIM: *Even though there is a big demand for autographed items for still-active stars, I don't recommend investing in them unless you're reasonably certain they have an excellent shot at Cooperstown (Henderson, Yount, Brett, for example).*

Jose Canseco, Bo Jackson, and Darryl Strawberry might all be HOF potential, but that is all. Potential. They will sign their names hundreds of thousands of times. Is it worth it to buy a $50 Bo Jackson autographed baseball? How much could that ball be worth in 20 years, especially if Bo Jackson is still signing? Ignorant investment capital is driving his market, much the way teenagers and dealers hype the market for current rookie cards.

Should you buy autographed items for retired players awaiting dead-certain enshrinement—Rod Carew, Mike Schmidt, Steve Carlton, Tom Seaver, and Reggie Jackson, to name the safest? Yes, because even though the supply may be plentiful, the demand will increase. Now, if you've already begun studying player access and demand, you'll know that Schmidt signatures are less plentiful than Jackson and Carlton, because Mike Schmidt hasn't put himself on the show circuit as often. He also hasn't begun merchandising himself like Steve Carlton, who sells his autographed bat for $130 (10 or more at $105 apiece). Why anyone would want an autographed bat of a pitcher (other than Babe Ruth, who pitched for a few seasons) is beyond me, especially from a player who regularly refused interviews for the last half of his career. Suddenly, Lefty wants to be noticed because he needs the money.

While you're leafing through SCD and other trade papers, you must make notes about which players are overexposed in the autograph-signing arena. In one issue of SCD, I noticed Robin Roberts was having a busy summer. He was appearing in Toledo, Ohio (autographed ball, $15), and Iowa City (ball, $12), among other places. This is known as an "easy" signature, and they have the least amount of investment potential. They may be famous, but the market will be flooded with their material should there be word of his serious illness and a subsequent rush to sell.

On the other hand, understand that today's huge signing business has caused a degree of hysterical overreaction in that certain high-demand players are not signing certain items anymore. This was best illustrated two years ago when Joe DiMaggio was scheduled to sign at a card show. There was a telling sentence that said Mr. DiMaggio would not sign baseballs. You can imagine what this did to the market for $50 single-signed DiMaggio balls. One dealer immediately placed an ad in SCD saying he'd buy as many as he could for $100. By attempting to corner the market on this item, the market value of a DiMag ball jumped to $150 to $175 overnight. DiMaggio also has personally informed me of his refusal to sign "anything in pinstripes," which I take to mean uniforms and photos where the famous Yankees pinstripes appear. I've seen ads from promoters that say, "Mr. DiMaggio will not sign bats." Obviously, no dealer or collector is happy about these restrictions, and most knowledgeable people in the business fear that it will only get worse. (I've seen signs at shows that say "no personalization," because the promoters don't want to slow down the assembly line at the signing factory. Some even say "no talking." This is ridiculous, and this kind of behavior poses a serious threat to the hobby.)

I cannot imagine their logic when players refuse to sign an object. Perhaps they feel dealers are making obscene profits on them, and they've decided to put an end to it. (Nobody accuses the players, however, of making obscene profits at shows.) But all they've really accomplished is to limit the supply and cause an unrealistically fast boost in price—and I think an unhealthy one—in the aftermarket trading of these particular goods.

It is well known throughout the business that Mickey Mantle has refused to sign bats, and speculation has it that Mantle wants to start an autographed-bat business. Why should he sell wholesale to dealers? His agent, Greer Johnson, probably thinks he could create an entire vertically integrated retail operation on his own. The Mantle autograph, like it or not, is an industry unto itself. All this has done is cause a hysterical demand for his signature on *any* Mantle-model bat. It is nearly impossible to find one for less than $1,000—even on a recently made "genuine" Mickey Mantle bat worth about $20. (See the detailed explanation about bats in Chapter 9.) Had you bought the bat at a sporting goods store before this restriction went into effect, you would have paid the Mantle promoters $35 for his signature at a show, and your $85 investment would have matured more than 10 times. (But how could you have known that? You couldn't. If you know someone who did it, he was lucky.)

This must be disillusioning news for anyone interested in collecting certain pieces of memorabilia—and it will probably have an overall adverse affect on the business—but there is nothing you can do about it except to hope to spot an early announcement of a player's signature restriction, and then rush to take advantage of it. You will also see some ludicrous— indeed, laughable—statements in ads, too. Imagine reading, "Mr. [Gregg] Jeffries no longer signs bats." It's true. All of 24 years old. Now, that's chutzpah in any language. Jose Canseco, I noticed in an SCD ad, also doesn't sign bats. Well, he's a better player than Jeffries, and he's a few years older. Draw your own conclusion about this display of arrogance. I'm assuming most of these advertising proclamations are true. If they're not, then the promoters should share some of the blame for making false claims.

MR. MINT'S MAXIM: *Do not speculate on rumor. Invest only in fact. Sooner or later, somebody will approach you at a baseball card show with a Hank Aaron autographed bat for a phenomenal amount of money. "You know Aaron is expected to stop signing bats soon, so this will double when the news gets out," he says. He may be right, and Aaron may be thinking that. But if Aaron changes his mind, you're out a lot of cash.*

You have probably come across the word "cut" in ads referring to autographs. A cut signature means the autograph is on a loose slip of paper that was scissored from a document. Usually these cuts came from a meaningless return letter to the person who requested an autograph, but they can be from a menu or a laundry list. Why people snip legitimate, famous autographs from even the least desirable document is a mystery to me. Most likely it is because they've heard that a personalized signature ("Best wishes to Harry Smith," for instance) devalues the autograph. In recent years, it has become fashionable for collectors and dealers to take these cut signatures, mat and mount them in handsome frames just below the player's photograph, and sell them, sometimes for unconscionably high prices.

In a recent visit to a card shop, I saw several of these pictures on the wall, some in color, some in black and white, yet all had cut signatures. Not a single player had signed the photo. A Roger Maris/Mickey Mantle photo, for example, was selling for $150. A good investment? No, it was severely overpriced. But a smart collector might pay $200 or $250 if the signatures were on the picture itself.

MR. MINT'S MAXIM: *Do not buy any item with a cut signature. In fact, do not buy any cut signatures at all. Ninety percent of the cut signatures I've seen are outright forgeries or impossible to verify. The first cousin of the cut signature is the autographed 3" by 5" index card. Avoid those for the same reason.*

Players' autographs on items such as checks, contracts, programs, yearbooks, postcards, and letters have become very desirable and collectible items. A canceled check is especially nice, because the bank theoretically has verified the signature by virtue of negotiating it. A postmark on a postcard helps the buyer determine authenticity, too. (See Chapter 12 on spotting fakes for a more detailed explanation.)

COLLECTING MEMORABILIA, PART 2: BALLS, BATS, UNIFORMS, GLOVES, AND SPIKES

The most cherished—and most valuable—collectibles to own are the personal pieces of a baseball player's career: the bats, balls, and the uniforms he wore.

Of these, the most popular and widely available items are autographed baseballs of Hall of Famers. There's something magical about grasping a major-league baseball, its perfect weight, its 108-stitch seams, and the friction you feel when you rub up the white horsehide like a relief pitcher contemplating a critical situation in the late innings. And when it has the signature of a Cobb, Ruth, Hornsby, Young, Alexander, Gehrig, or a Walter Johnson on it, you now have something in your hands that is no longer just a baseball, but something special, a small stitch in the fabric of American history.

The vogue in autographed baseballs is the single-signature ball. To collect an entire set of HOFers is a daunting, frightfully expensive, and probably impossible task, but some people out there are attempting it. (Signatures of some HOF old-timers are extremely rare on any item—Candy Cummings, John Clarkson, Henry Chadwick, and Ed Delahanty, to name four—and it's not known whether single-signed balls by those players even exist.) What makes it so difficult is that 50 years ago and more, there wasn't a collector's wont to get a ball signed by only one player. On the contrary, baseball fans (remember, the fan existed far earlier than the collector) gathered and crowded as many signatures as possible on a single ball. A ball signed by Babe Ruth, Connie Mack, and Cy Young—all very famous HOFers— sold in 1990 for $4,675 at auction. But collectors would prefer having three individual balls signed by each of those great names, which would cost much more than the three-signature ball.

MR. MINT'S MAXIM: *While there is nothing wrong with a ball signed by Ty Cobb and a bunch of unknown Detroit Tigers on his team, remember that it is much less valuable than a ball signed by Cobb alone.*

The lone possible exception to this theory is the Babe Ruth/ Lou Gehrig ball. Both players were so legendary that their signatures on a ball are worth a lot of money either individually or together. Which single-signed ball is worth more money? If you guessed Lou Gehrig, you're correct. Ruth balls hover in the $3,000 to $5,000 range, depending on condition (an absolutely spectacular specimen does sell for more), but a beautiful single-signed Gehrig ball is easily worth $12,000 to $15,000. The simple reason is rarity. The Babe was extremely accessible and generous with his autograph, and there are reports that he signed many thousands of balls in his long career, and thousands more after he retired. I've seen old newsreels where the Sultan of Swatt is stepping out of cabs signing a bucket full of balls and then handing them out to kids. Gehrig was more reserved off the field, and he signed balls much more sparingly. I've seen literally hundreds of Ruth balls as a dealer; perhaps only two or three Gehrig balls.

Though Gehrig and Ruth were not the closest of teammates, they respected each other and Gehrig understood his number two spot behind Ruth in the pantheon of Yankees tradition. When both were asked to sign balls, Gehrig always left the sweet spot to Ruth. Only when Ruth retired did Gehrig sign on the sweet spot.

When a collector showed me a ball that had both Jackie Robinson's and Willie Mays' autographs, he was amazed and nearly insulted when I told him it would have been worth a lot more money had Mays not signed it. Why? First, Mays is alive and he signs incessantly at shows. Two, Robinson and Mays have absolutely nothing noteworthy in common (other than being great ball players, black, and in the HOF). A single-signed Robinson ball is worth $2,500 to $3,000. Mays made the ball worth perhaps $1,000 or $1,500. This collector, had he added a few more HOF signatures, would have had the beginning of what I call a mish-mosh ball, and Robinson's rare, coveted signature would have decreased even further.

MR. MINT'S MAXIM: *Mish-mosh signature balls are extremely common, and they are wonderful mementos, but they have limited appeal and, hence, limited investment value when compared with single-signed balls and theme balls. The value of these balls is strictly determined by the number of well-recognized stars or HOF players. So when you see three of four famous names on a ball from a Japanese tour, contain yourself and look for something more meaningful.*

Like a theme ball. Theme balls include those autographed by an entire team, an All-Star game ball, or a group of players who are related in some way by their contribution to baseball history. Balls with the signatures of Roger Maris and Mickey Mantle, the 1927 or 1961 Yankees, the 1955 Dodgers, the 1954 Giants, or the 1960 Pirates (all World Series winners), or balls with 300-game winners, 500-home-run hitters, Cy Young Award winners, or MVP award winners have a significance that gives them desirability and value. A 1934 All-Star American League team ball that included signatures of Ruth, Gehrig, Fox, Simmons, and Cronin (whom Carl Hubbell struck out in succession) is a rare and desired ball. I sold one for $7,000. I've seen baseballs with Tinker, Evers, and Chance on them, but they've had other signatures, too. A ball signed by just those three players would probably be worth $15,000 to $20,000.

I'd pay dearly, and so would collectors, for the ultimate theme ball of Ruth, Cobb, Wagner, Mathewson, and Johnson. Does one exist? The likelihood is next to nil, because Christie Mathewson died in 1925, 11 years before these five immortals were the first HOF designees. Nobody could have anticipated their commonality before Matty died.

But let's confine ourselves to collecting the obtainable, like a 1969 Mets ball or any World Series championship team ball. For instance, suppose you were looking at a St. Louis 1964 team ball, a year where the Cardinals beat the Yankees in the World Series. This is not in significantly large demand (except among St. Louis area collectors, I assume), so it's probably worth only $200 or $300 in top condition. A complete signature ball (everyone on the roster) is the one that will bring the most money. If it's missing a coach or two, or a reserve player who pitched only an inning or two or was used as a pinch runner, then it's not a horrible devaluation. But it must contain the names of all the starters, especially the stars: Bob Gibson, Curt Flood, Lou Brock, Ken Boyer, Dick Groat, Tim McCarver, Ray Sadecki, Roger Craig.

One of the most sought-after team balls is that of the 1927 Yankees, considered by many historians and experts to be the greatest club that ever took the field. Whether it's true is a matter that has been—and will be—debated in saloons forever. The perception is what counts as far as collecting is concerned. And that is why a 1927 team ball sells for double or triple the Yankees 1926 or 1928 ball, even though the rosters were virtually identical. So, how can you tell the difference between a 1926, 1927, and 1928 Yankees ball? There are two minor members, a pitcher named Joe Giard and a coach, Julie Werer, who were on the 1927 roster but were not in 1926 or 1928. In order to make these determinations, you must consult a book like the *Sports Encyclopedia of Baseball* (St. Martin's Press), an excellent reference work if you're buying team balls. It gives complete rosters, including coaches. (The *Baseball Encyclopedia* accounts for every player who ever appeared in a game, but it does not give complete team rosters on a year-by-year basis.)

MR. MINT'S MAXIM: *Do not invest in autographed balls with only a couple of famous players that are padded with a lot of unknown players. (If they're unknown to you, they probably will be unknown to a potential buyer when you want to sell it.)*

It's difficult to accurately assess the worth of many multi-player signed baseballs. Remember, any defect, physical or psychological, should devalue it as an investment. If American League players have signed a National League official ball, then begin subtracting.

If an autographed ball isn't an official one (it has the stamped signature of the league president), it's worth significantly less—20 to 30 percent or more. A dealer I know had a Babe Ruth signature on a ball which was manufactured by a company I had never heard of. It probably was a ball sold in five-and-dime stores.

Though the ball was in near mint condition, and the signature was bold and dark, the ball was worth less than half of what it would have been on an official ball. Nonofficial balls (I call them Gillette balls because companies put their stamps on them for promotional consideration) proliferate, so always check stamping.

After balls, the other item that has become the rage of the collecting world is the baseball bat. At every show I attend, there are growing hordes of collectors with bags of bats slung over their shoulder, waiting on line for an autograph. At its most inexpensive level, collectors are spending $100 to $200 and more for bats that are signed by current players, recently retired stars, or living HOFers. In the vast majority of these cases, serious collectors and top-level dealers feel that these people are naively overpaying for an autograph on a cheap-grade bat known as a store-model bat because it is sold to the public through sporting goods outlets.

Let me explain. The autograph part of the industry is in such a frenzy that the average, unseasoned collector (and dealer) think that if Willie Stargell's autograph is worth $15 on a photo and $20 on a ball, then it must be worth $75 to $100 if it's on a Stargell-model bat. These folks have no inkling at all that there are thousands of these bats, and they were not made exclusively for Willie Stargell (he's a retired player and a HOFer, remember?), but for the public at large. The bats were *recently* manufactured, or newly minted, in the lowest-grade ash, and Stargell never touched them. Only his agent and the bat company may know they exist.

MR. MINT'S MAXIM: *Signed store bats of living players are a trap and have limited investment potential for the long term. Sooner or later, the market will be flooded with them, and collectors will find they've painfully overpaid for the autograph that appears on them.*

I may be wrong on this theory, but if you decide to speculate in these relatively low-priced signed bats, make sure you are aware of what you are buying. Often, you will come across store-model bats of older, more famous players, or deceased ones. I saw numerous examples of Robinson bats with the Hillerich & Bradsby label, the "Genuine Louisville Slugger" on the barrel with the Jackie Robinson facsimile autograph etched in it. "JR4" or "JR5" was on the heel of the knob. The bats were nice-looking, nearly new, in fact. They were not autographed and they were selling for about $200. The unsuspecting collector might think these were bats that Robinson had in the Brooklyn bat rack at one time during his career, even though they didn't have any wear. That is, nobody is making any claims that they were game-used.

But astute readers of SCD would have clipped Michael Montbriand's occasional "Gone Bats" columns, which provide a detailed analysis of bat pedigree, and discovered that the labels indicated the Robinsons were made sometime between 1965 and 1972. Robinson played his last game in 1956. It may have been an "official" bat, but it was merely an official facsimile and not Jackie's own. I painstakingly point this out because one model was offered at a West Coast auction as an "unused vintage bat," which may have misled many unsuspecting bidders. It sold for $209 (auction estimate $100 to $125). The other one I saw was owned by a card shop owner who suspected it was only a store model—it "looked too new" to be a Robinson bat—and he had no idea how much to sell it for.

In that same auction, there was another Jackie Robinson bat, this one with a detailed description along with two photos of it. The catalog copy read:

> Jackie Robinson signed in black ink "Best Wishes, Jackie Robinson" on his game-used model Hillerich & Bradsby "Louisville Slugger" with "JR5" on knob, a lovely classic piece of lumber of the most important figure in the game's history, signature is a solid "9," rare ....estimate, $7,000–$8,000.

The bat looked exactly like the other unsigned Robinson in the catalog, but this one—though it sounded exciting, even downright mouth-watering—looked too new to be "game-used." I had someone call the auction house before the sale, and an employee checked the two bats and said they were exactly alike. So I knew the bat couldn't possibly be game-used, unless Jackie used it (nine years after he retired, and possibly as long as 16 years—he died in 1972) to hit the ball around somebody's backyard. Bat expert Michael Montbriand apparently noticed this, too, and he informed the auction house before the sale. The description was amended before the bat went on the block. But some bidder paid $5,500 for it anyway, based solely on the fact that Robinson's autograph (on anything) is rare and worth a considerable amount of money.

Was it worth it? I'm not certain. Any Robinson-engraved bat with Robinson's signature might actually be worth that much to some collectors, and it might escalate in value. The point of this tale, however, is to illustrate how easy it is for even an auctioneer, dealer, or any memorabilia expert to be mistaken.

There is a midstage type of bat called a coach's bat, which is, in fact, officially manufactured for retired ball players who still have a job with a major-league club. These are not playing-era bats, however, and should not command the same prices that those do. Special-issue, "World Series," or commemorative bats are a level more desirable than store bats, but they only take on real value when autographed. The same thing is true with "team" bats, made for National League pitchers or coaches, but not a specific player.

If you get into the "game-used" bat market, you are swimming with the sharks. Bats virtually all look alike but they are very complicated items, and one of the keys to understanding them is to try to find out as much about them as you can before you write a four-figure check and regret it.

A new collector called me to ask my advice on whether he should buy a game-used Mike Schmidt bat. Everything about the bat looked okay, he said. It was a black Adirondack, just the kind Schmidt used. It had his uniform number on the knob and his name etched on the barrel. What bothered the collector was that it was taped on the handle. Didn't Schmidt use pine tar and batting gloves? I didn't remember, so I asked the obvious question: Does it come with a letter of authenticity? The collector went back to the dealer. It did not. The dealer explained that he bought it from another dealer who had previously acquired it from a respected collector who was extremely careful about buying genuine goods. This is not enough, however. If the dealer was so certain of its provenance, why didn't he obtain invoices or letters from the previous owners?

MR. MINT'S MAXIM: *Caveat emptor. It is very difficult to verify a bat actually used by a player in a major-league game. (Was it scuffed at a softball game last week? Did the player himself use it, or did one of his teammates? Was it used only in batting practice? Often, players themselves cannot remember which stick they used.) If you invest in one of these bats, deal only with a dealer who is an expert in the area and insist on written documentation. Reliable dealers usually get these items from unimpeachable sources—the player's attorney or agent, a family member, the clubhouse attendant, or a batboy.*

In addition, find out as much as you can about the player's habits involving his bats. Some players used cupped bats (hollowed at the end, they are lighter and afford greater bat speed), some used black Adirondacks only, some changed. Some players switched bats frequently, others used their bats until they cracked or "ran out of hits."

If it's a major investment—a signed Mickey Mantle bat, for

instance—then you should consider paying for an outside appraisal from a bona fide bat dealer. According to Montbriand, Mantle used several different models (including both Hillerich & Bradsby and Adirondack) throughout his career, usually alternating different sticks even in a game where he hit from both sides of the plate. Mantle's signature jumped to $900 to $1,000 last year on *any* bat, because in 1989 he decided not to sign them anymore. A game-used *unsigned* Mantle bat sold for $5,600; obviously a signed gamer would bring more. Mike Schmidt's game-used bats are surfacing because of his indisputable HOF credentials (he reportedly doesn't sign bats anymore either). Unsigned game-used Schmidt bats were selling for $600 to $700—double what they were a year before—and signed ones reached $1,000.

I do not mean to sound overly alarmist about this phase of the business, but somebody has to temper the impatient, hysterical craving for these often nongenuine items.

A few other things you should know before you buy any bats. I come from the strict and conservative school of thought surrounding any antique. I feel an objet d'art should remain in the condition in which it was found. Any restoration is usually a bad idea and has the potential to make it worse than it was. There is some disagreement within the business about whether a "cracked and restored" bat is more desirable than one that is merely "cracked." (A cracked or damaged bat, however, is definitely not worth as much as one that is merely "used.") Montbriand has had several nonrestored cracked bats for many years. After a while, he says, the wood begins to expand and eventually it falls apart. You might as well throw it away. He feels strongly that a properly restored cracked bat will be a lasting collectible, especially if the work is done skillfully enough as to be unnoticeable. Obviously, a cracked and restored bat, no matter how expertly restored, should be so identified. If you buy a restored bat, be certain the barrel is smooth; it shouldn't still be splintered in any way.

Montbriand makes one other interesting point about cracked bats. He feels this is the only type of bat that is certain beyond doubt to be game-used. What dealer or unscrupulous seller is willing to try and pass off a $40 facsimile by attempting to crack it as if game-damaged? It's apparently not that easy to fake a crack, though I'm willing to bet that after reading some of Montbriand's articles, somebody will try it.

Finally, you should know that the most common writing instrument for autographing nonblack bats is the blue felt-tip Sharpie pen (silver or gold on a black bat). It gives a smooth, lush result, and when it dries it doesn't smudge. However, Montbriand noticed that after a period of years, blue Sharpie signatures begin fading into a light turquoise. It's his opinion that they could eventually disappear, or at least become so light they will be difficult to read or become unattractive. The solution is simple.

MR. MINT'S MAXIM: *If you've bought a star's bat and want to upgrade it at an autograph signing, bring a black Sharpie pen. It won't fade.*

As you become more experienced in memorabilia, you will undoubtedly notice there is a rising amount of interest in shirts and warm-up jackets, especially if it can be confirmed that they were worn or used by the player. Again, authenticating whether some item of clothing is actually game-worn is a difficult task, especially since three of four people actually claimed they owned Pete Rose game-used jerseys from his record-setting 4,193-hit game. Rose apparently changed his shirt in the clubhouse between innings, certainly an enterprising idea but one which will continue to cast doubts among serious collectors if the trend persists. (Let's hope Rickey Henderson doesn't change his cleats every inning when he steals his 939th base.

He should have easily broken the record by the time this book is in print.)

We can't blame Rose completely for this kind of desperation. At the 1990 All-Star game in Chicago, collectors besieged the players at their hotel with every kind of item imaginable, hungry for autographs. Players who are confronted by someone with a dozen baseball caps are rightfully suspicious of the signature-seeker's motives. The righteous players feel that one signature or two is enough for a collector. Any more, and they're thinking immediate resale. (There's no age minimum for dealers, you know.)

MR. MINT'S MAXIM: *If you venture into the jersey market, you must be just as vigilant and knowledgeable as if you were buying bats. Perhaps more. The number of forged jerseys has increased so much in the past few years that one prominent dealer became so disillusioned he stopped buying and selling them. If you are buying the shirt of a real player, be as certain as you can you're buying the shirt off his back.*

Jerseys, or the top half of a player's uniform, come in all kinds of styles. There are home and away shirts (the home one is usually worth more), some are zippered, and some are buttoned, and some like the old Pirates uniforms are sleeveless. The older uniforms are large, bulky flannels, while the modern counterparts are the lighter, airier knits. Many of today's players have names sewn above the number, and some may think this is an added piece of nostalgia, but you'll never convince me that C-A-N-S-E-C-O on the back of an Oakland A's shirt is a better investment than an old Yankees pinstripe with a number 3, 4, 5, or 7 on the back.

Do not get caught on the modern, current-player knit merry-go-round because there are so many of these things popping up. One dealer confided, "You have no idea how many collectors have told me they have a game-worn Clemens or Boggs uniform from 1985. It's hard to believe these guys had 75 different jerseys that year. They may not have had that many in their whole careers."

An ad in SCD listed 60 or so "game-worn jerseys," ranging in price from $70 (an unidentified Red Sox player's road uniform number 6, no year given, faded) to $495 (Bruce Sutter's 1985 road uniform). Why anyone would pay $185 for Joe Beckwith's shirt or $199 for Thad Bosley's is a complete mystery to me, yet these jerseys were also on the slate. Card and hobby stores are selling so many uniforms ("reproductions," not unlike store bats), and so many collectors are getting them signed, that there is bound to be mass confusion about what's real. The major-league baseball trademark regularly appears on new-issue articles of clothing, which merely means the licensing agreement has been legally struck. One company has the license to make facsimiles of major-league jerseys—you see fans wearing them at games all the time. There is nothing to stop anyone from trying to put a player's forged signature on it and asking $400 or $500. So, caveat emptor.

Again, is it worth it to invest $300 in a signed Jose Canseco uniform that is an obvious reproduction? Probably not. Let's say Jose signs only hundreds of these, not thousands. And let's give the Oakland slugger the benefit of all doubt and assume he'll make the HOF in 20 years. If you still have it in 2011, maybe you'll get $3,000 for it. There are far safer, better investments than the shirt that's (not) off Canseco's back.

It is far less risky to try to obtain items that are not as likely to be reproduced, altered, and disputed as jerseys. Signed batting gloves, a pair of spikes (base stealers are preferred, like Lou Brock, Rickey Henderson, Vince Coleman), and hats can be bought for well under four figures, sometimes under three figures, unless the item is very old and rare. Ty Cobb's shoes, of course, would bring several thousand, as would any item that is likely to be coveted by the curator in Cooperstown. Be aware that the batting glove is a relatively new phenomenon, even though few of today's players leave the dugout without them. If someone is peddling Luke Appling's batting glove, or his batting helmet, common sense should dictate that something like this is an impossible item.

A relatively new, somewhat undiscovered autograph idea appears to be the team-signed glove. A child's mitt signed by 29 players from the 1969 Mets brought over $3,000 at auction, far higher than an equivalent baseball. One reason, I suspect, is that the player autographs were dark, large, and much more readable than if they had been on a ball. Gil Hodges, the Mets manager, signed this one in the pocket. Also, the spirited bidding on the glove was due to the fact that collectors immediately took notice of its rarity. If you're musing about a team-signed item of a famous club, one signature at a time, it costs only $30 or $40 for a decent adult-sized glove, so it's not a bad idea—although gathering the autographs is sure to take a lot of legwork. Again, you're better off waiting for an old one, preferably complete or missing only a few signatures, of a team 20 years old plus. But beware, there were a lot of school kids daydreaming in class who could have signed the player's name on his official glove. There's a greater degree of unintentional forgeries with gloves than with other items.

COLLECTING MEMORABILIA,
PART 3: MISCELLANEOUS MATTER

I've always considered baseball collectors to be among the strangest of animals. Their imaginations have no boundaries. At the 1990 National Convention, a collector and a colleague, dealer Joshua Evans, didn't let me down. Evans bought a vial of dirt from Ebbets Field from a collector he called "years ahead of his time." He paid $500 for this tiny piece of what was once terra firma on the hallowed Brooklyn ball field, scooped for posterity on April 9, 1960. Evans said that he turned down an immediate $600 resale; he wanted to display it in his office. ("This is true. I swear it," he wrote in SCD.)

No mention was made of authenticity, but my guess is that Evans didn't care whether this vial of dirt came with a letter and photo from a groundskeeper swearing on a Bible that it was freshly dug up near second base. He's already received his $500 worth of publicity. I am certainly a great believer in publicity—for the hobby, as well as my own business—but I don't think I'll ever buy dirt from any ball park.

Though I would never in my most capricious mood ever advise a client to invest in baseball field dirt, it illustrates my point that someone out there will buy just about anything remotely related to our great American pastime. (I would not be surprised if I saw an ad in SCD for an autographed, "guaranteed prison-worn" Pete Rose denim with his federal number, 01832-061, sewn on the breast. Comes with letter of authenticity from a prison guard at Marion, Illinois. You're smiling? This is the same guy who was hawking his merchandise on cable TV the night after he was banned from baseball. A lot of folks wouldn't put such a stunt past Charlie Hustle, and even if it were a hoax, somebody out there would send a check.)

In this chapter I'd like to alert you to some of the more narrow but stable venues of baseball collectibility, especially those with better investment value than Ebbets Field dirt. They include programs, scorecards, newspapers, books, and magazines, HOF postcards (known as "plaques"), tickets and stubs, stadium seats, press pins, season passes, advertising pieces, proof sheets, pennants, and uncut sheets of baseball cards. Other than very old press pins and the rarest of famous-player advertising pieces, seldom do these items cost more than a few hundred dollars. There are excellent opportunities for under a hundred, too.

The buy (or resale) market here is perhaps smaller than for jerseys, bats, and balls, but it's continually strong because the collectors are serious and knowledgeable. I recommend you acquaint yourself with the following:

Press pins. Newsmen who covered the World Series beginning in 1911, and the All-Star game in 1938, were issued official lapel pins by home teams. The early World Series pins consisted of ribbons and medals, and then enamel buttons became standard. They vary in degree of attractiveness; some are ornate, others are simple designs. Rarity, naturally, plays a big part in price, but aesthetics and the reputation of the given team are the dominant factors.

The better-looking ones cost more, the same as with an antique piece of furniture. You'll see all kinds of conditions, but hold out for near mint, because they're well made, were usually worn for less than a week, and then were put away in boxes. The 1938 Cubs World Series pin is a beautiful design of a forlorn-looking bear cub "holding" a ball. It is highly sought after by pin collectors, not only in Chicago but everywhere. The 1938 Cubs pin and the 1927 Yankees pin have recently fetched $3,500 to $4,000. The losing team usually costs less than the champion's version. Here is an extremely *rough* idea of what the terrain is like should you become interested in investing in World Series pins:

> 1980–91: $50–$100
> 1970–79: $100–$200
> 1960–69: $200–$500
> 1950–59: $150–$400
> 1940–49: $500–$1,000
> 1930–39: $1,000–$3,000
> 1920–29: $3,000–$5,000
> 1911–19: $5,000–$35,000

MR. MINT'S MAXIM: *Beware of reproductions (they cost $5 to $10): they're easy to spot because of their gloss and newness. Beckett's collectibles price guide contains an illustration for each original pin, and I suggest you study it before you make any purchases. The guide also meticulously describes the type of clasp used on each issue. HOF induction ceremony press pins dating from 1982 are numbered.*

Ticket stubs. Ticket stubs from early World Series games are very collectible right now; they appear to be immune from the recession that causes middle-condition goods to be devalued.

From the 1950s onward, I feel they're slightly overvalued. People were well aware of their collectibility and began squirreling them away by the boxload. Begin a collection prior to 1950, if you can afford it. A 1969 World Series stub from Shea Stadium sold for $95 at a New York City auction (below the $125 to $150 estimate), which suggests that collectors are wising up to the plentiful supply of these items. The best stubs are from championship games, old-timers games, and All-Star games. Negro-leagues tickets are very collectible and in demand.

Regular-season games are only desirable if the ticket represents a significant performance. In 1990, for example, tickets from Nolan Ryan's sixth no-hitter against the A's were a big item. The Oakland box office was inundated by collectors the following day with inquiries to purchase tickets from the game. (None were sold, but if the A's management didn't destroy all of them, expect a few to begin surfacing on the market.) Other significant tickets are the last game at the Polo Grounds and the first game at Yankee Stadium. Be aware that these tickets are often overvalued, and there are many around because everyone knew in advance about the game's significance. How many people do you think kept their stubs from the 1990 final game at Comiskey Park? Almost everyone in the crowd of 43,931. I'll wager that collectors and dealers were buying up stubs at the game, not to mention those who purchased a box-seat block of four and didn't use two or three seats.

A 1949 Yankees ticket for a regular-season game now runs about $30 to $40, and there's no reason why you should pay that much. These should cost much, much less. If you had a ticket for Jackie Robinson's first major-league game, that would be significant.

Thankfully, stubs are one kind of cardboard that do not bear the same degree of microscopic condition scrutiny as a baseball card. There are really only two conditions: very worn, heavily creased (poor to fair) and anything above that (very good to excellent or better). A full unused ticket goes for substantially more money than the torn stub.

MR. MINT'S MAXIM: *Do not buy old tickets unless they have seat numbers. Those without numbers are artist's proofs, and they're virtually worthless. The seat numbers are usually printed in a different-color ink in a separate press run. Many of these numberless tickets are around from the 1940s and 1950s, and they're often peddled in large blocks.*

Phantoms. You will see World Series press pins and tickets that are known as phantoms in the hobby because of teams that were scheduled to show up in the Fall Classic but didn't win their respective pennants. If the league race was at all close in late August or early September, the front office of a contender was forced to go to the expense of printing tickets and ordering pins. The 1954 Brooklyn Dodgers expected to be playing at Ebbets Field, but Leo Durocher's Giants spoiled their plans. Hence, the 1954 phantom Dodger tickets. Obviously, phantoms are not stubs. There were a lot of close races in baseball history, so expect to find phantoms of any of those runners-up. Treat these as very desirable items.

HOF postcards. Commonly known as plaques, these post-cards are sold at the gift shop at the Hall of Fame in Cooperstown. After the Albertype Company of Brooklyn began printing the cards in 1936, collectors began asking the players to autograph them. Today, they're extremely popular.

Understand the brief history of plaques. Albertype made the black and white ones until 1952, when the firm was bought by Artvue Postcard Company of New York. Artvue continued printing them in black and white until 1964. In 1964 the HOF began selling the now-familiar brown and yellow cards made by two companies, Curteichcolor and Mike Roberts Color Productions. (In 1980, Dexter Press published a run of plaques in orange, green, blue, and red. They did not catch on with the hobbyists, however, and only hard-core postcard collectors, who must have a complete set of every one made, seek them. Don't bother with them.)

Basically, there are two groups of plaques commonly found at shows; the black and white Artvues and the brown-and-yellows. White Artvues are highly desired and difficult to find. The yellows are plentiful. If you're thinking of investing or collecting plaques, I would begin with the more difficult Artvues and pretty much avoid the yellows. The complete Artvue set, unsigned, is worth about $500, and it's a nice collection for someone who is beginning in the hobby with a limited budget.

MR. MINT'S MAXIM: *If you're buying signed plaques, make sure you only invest in those with signatures at the top or bottom of the card. I once paid $500 for a Jimmy Foxx Albertype that was signed across the plaque. The signature was quite readable, but it was in the "wrong" spot for the majority of collectors.*

Stadium seats. Nearly everyone who is touched by this hobby someday covets owning a seat from his favorite ballpark. Obviously, it's difficult to put together something called a collection unless you have a huge garage or rent a warehouse to store it. The high-demand seats usually come from defunct ballparks like the Polo Grounds and Ebbets Field, and Yankee Stadium has its own special aura. They usually come in three shapes: single, double, and quad, and the price escalates with the number of actual chairs.

MR. MINT'S MAXIM: *Some seats are repainted and restored, and in my opinion, great for watching a game in your den but poor as an investment. If you buy one in very worn shape, leave it that way (and don't sit in it) if you ever want to resell it.*

My sense is that the seats in Charlie Comiskey's 80-year-old park will be a wonderful item, and not just among Chicago collectors. When it closed its gates for good at the end of 1990, it held the record for the oldest continuously used ballpark in the major leagues (1910 to 1990, a pretty good run). This was the house, after all, where the infamous Black Sox threw the 1919 World Series. Seats, bricks (will they be more precious than a vial of dirt?), and other parts of the facility that were deemed salvageable were first offered to season ticket holders. Ballpark seats are difficult to authenticate, so if some of those season ticket holders are reselling theirs in the hobby market, you should ask for a photocopy of their White Sox receipts. If they match the box-seat number, you know you have a real item. (Expect to find a lot of paraphernalia from every corner of Comiskey Park for sale. In 1990, well before the White Sox played their final game, park officials reported that fans were already stealing anything remotely collectible. They had done everything but rip out the seats, and it was expected that those would go, too. Two men were even arrested in the middle of the night attempting to steal—honest to God—home plate. While I was preparing this book, I noticed a news story saying that White Sox officials were already in dispute with the salvage company over who owned the rights to the "fixtures.")

Seats are in a bull market, for some unfathomable reason. Yankee Stadium seats were $300 apiece and $600 for a double, and the price had been rock-steady until the end of 1990. Then prices abruptly doubled. The asking price for a pair of Ebbets Field seats in near mint condition at that time was $2,000.

There is, as you might have guessed, a text for seat collectors. *Ballparks of North America: A Comprehensive Reference to Baseball Grounds, Yards, and Stadiums, 1845 to Present,* by Michael Benson, was published in 1990. The 475-page illustrated book lists every field used for organized baseball since the sport's inception.

Scorecards, yearbooks, and programs. These are the ultimate ballpark souvenirs, and fans have faithfully tucked them away in their drawers and closets for the greater part of this century. The ones from the 1930s and 1940s have beautifully illustrated covers, unlike many of the ugly ones done for today's gamegoers. They often appear in very nice condition, and there's no reason to settle for anything less than excellent to mint. Autographs on scorecards, yearbooks, or commemorative programs (World Series, old-timers, or All-Star games) will enhance their value.

Unscored programs tend to be preferable to hobbyists who insist on quality condition, but I think a neatly filled-in box score, especially those where the attendance, umpires, and time of the game are listed, enhances them as a collector's item. Unless the scorecard is horribly scribbled or doodled, don't think a scored program is undesirable. The early programs are excellent investments, though they can be quite expensive. In the summer of 1990 I auctioned a 1934 St. Louis World Series program for $760 and a 1928 Yankees one for $1,210. The 1931 St. Louis program went for $370.

There are lots of yearbooks available, and the prices vary with age and rarity. Most teams' yearbooks from the 1960s onward can be collected in the under $100 range. It's only when you get as far back as the 1950s that they become scarcer and more expensive.

Uncut sheets and proof sheets. In the past few years, the printer's proof sheets and uncut sheets of cards have surfaced on the collectibles market (especially those from 1970s and 1980s issues). So many have come up for sale that it could certainly make a collector suspicious about the card company's motives. How do they manage to so conveniently slip out the door of the manufacturing plants? Employee theft? Are they subtle public relations gambits? Does an executive bring one home for his kid's birthday? Since baseball cards are manufactured in very large lots, the uncut sheets tend to be unwieldly and difficult to keep in top-grade condition. Since many are too big for framing, they are bought and sold in rolled-up form. The corners and edges often become creased. Cards in uncut sheets are highly desired by collectors, who will often pay a large premium over the mint book price of the sum of the cards, especially if there are star or rookie players in them. They can cost as much as two or three times what the cards themselves would normally cost.

MR. MINT'S MAXIM: *Don't buy uncut cards or sheets unless there is at least one star featured, preferably two or three. An uncut sheet of all common players (unless it is very old, rare, and in mint condition) is just that. Common.*

Don't confuse uncut card sheets with proof sheets, which come on plastic-coated paper (not unlike the stock glossy magazines are printed on). The purpose of the proof is to give the printer and his client an idea of what the final result will look like. When proofs are pulled, the company's art production manager can then make specific changes. They are rarer and tougher to find than the cards themselves, because there are usually only four or five proofs pulled per given card sheet. Only the last sheet pulled is close to perfect, and it's impossible to tell unless it's numbered ("proof #5," for example). Whether it's numbered depends on the proclivities of the printer. And even when they're numbered, there's no way of telling how many proofs he made. Remember, the printer is not thinking about their collectible value. He's worried about whether the ink is running. So the colors in early proofs are occasionally out of register, or slightly smeared due to overinking. A proof sheet also has color bars, which are usually visible on one or more edges. Of course, the more carefully it's trimmed, the better it is.

MR. MINT'S MAXIM: *Do not invest in any proof sheet with serious printing flaws, even if there's a Mickey Mantle card in it. One reason it will be offered at such a bargain-basement price is its poor condition. (It was meant to be thrown away in the first place.)*

Hartland statues and Bobbin' Head dolls. In an earlier chapter I expressed my reluctance to recommend investing in any current figurines and recently manufactured merchandise. The only two *possible* exceptions are the Hartland plastic statues produced from 1958 to 1963 and the Bobbin' Head dolls from the 1960s. I still can't understand the mentality of the Bobbin' Head collectors; they're animated look-alikes of star players. Those readers who are over 40 probably remember when people once put them in the rear windows of their cars. Personally, I think they're horrible caricatures of the players, and I suppose their collectible appeal began as a goof.

The Hartlands, at least, are not so repugnant-looking, and collectors covet them even though they're made of plastic. I suppose even semi-attractive items begin to have an appeal after they're aged 30 years or so. If you must bite for the Hartlands, there are 18 in all (Colavito, Aaron, Banks, Drysdale, Groat, Killebrew, Nellie Fox, Mantle, Berra, Mays, Ted Williams, Snider, Ruth, Mathews, Musial, Maris, Aparicio, and Spahn). The toughest Hartlands are the Colavito, Groat, and Killebrew because they were made in the fewest number. The Spahn and the Ruth are the most common ones. Condition varies greatly and so do the prices. A complete iceberg-white set could run $6,000, while a yellowed version might only bring $1,000. Stay away from the reproduction series, which sell for $25 to $30 apiece.

Pennants. Other than the baseball card itself, it's difficult to think of a better example of American adolescent male iconography. Baseball pennants anointed the walls of the rooms of boys growing up in America since they were first made. They still do. These felt collectibles were dirt-cheap at issue, and you probably can't remember how many times you brought one home from the souvenir stand at the ballpark only to tack it (ouch) to your wall. No wonder the old, very rare ones usually come with pin or nail holes.

Current pennants are made in massive quantities, so do not look for investment-grade pennants after the 1960s. Sure, they'll increase in value but at a very slow pace. The old, well-preserved pennants, especially of well-known World Series teams or other commemoratives, are the best buys. My suggestion would be to invest in just a few hard-to-get pennants, rather than any long runs of less expensive ones. Nobody has any idea how many of these were produced.

Baseball board games. It seemed that every year or so an enterprising manufacturer came up with another notion for a board game. Then, too, player endorsements were less expensive to obtain by promoters, and they tended to sell their approval to anyone with a scheme and some ready cash. All sorts of failed enterprises come under the collectible umbrella here, because when a game wasn't popular, it was usually abandoned, and the unsold inventory was destroyed.

The games that survived the incinerator, especially those from the 1920s or 1930s, are only worth buying if they are in excellent or better condition (no pieces missing, if possible, and no serious flaws like torn cardboard boxes), and only if there is a star player endorsement (Babe Ruth, Christy Mathewson, or the equivalent).

Magazines, newspapers, and other miscellaneous items. Even new collectors are surprised to see how little time it takes to come across an old advertising piece or a set of *Street & Smith's Baseball* magazines or a player's inscribed cigarette lighter or an ashtray from a World Series winner. It wasn't long ago when Gillette seemed to have cornered the market on the baseball greats. And as late as the 1950s, players regularly endorsed cigarettes.

A good general rule is to steer clear of the magazines and newspapers unless they contain rare autographs of stars, simply because there are so many of them around. Everybody's grandmother kept the stuff; it's fragile and it's often yellowed or crumpled. Even very old magazines and famous player-authored "how-to-play-ball" books from the 1920s and 1930s are ubiquitous items. Issues of *Sporting News, Sports Illustrated, Sport,* and other publications just don't stand to increase in value at an acceptable pace. One reason is that it's so difficult to assemble a complete set.

You've just spotted a picture of DiMaggio on the cover of an old issue of *Life,* signed at last month's auction by Joltin' Joe. These kinds of things are constantly for sale for $150 and more and are usually bad buys. People with framed magazine photos and illustrations will always be selling their stuff for more than it's worth at almost any card show. Before you marvel at the folklore, remember it's a piece of paper printed many thousands of times (sometimes, in the case of *Time, Life,* or *Look,* hundreds of thousands or millions of times), and it just happens to have a signature (of a living player).

MR. MINT'S MAXIM: *If you're going to take a flier on a baseball doodad of some sort you've never seen, try to stick to a one-of-a-kind item.*

Pedigree or provenance can also be very important to an item's future worth. If an item is inscribed by a famous player to someone who is also famous (say, Gehrig signed a picture for a movie star), it's all the more desirable. If the piece was in a famous collection, then it will command more money.

You have to trust your experience and investment instincts when you see the great dearth of these items in stores, shows, and on the auction block. If you see a lot of something, you know not to pounce. When you find a one-of-a-kind item, reach for your checkbook. As you become more involved, you'll begin to define your own parameters of scarcity on unclassified baseball collectibles, and you will begin to accrue more knowledge than the average dealer.

AUCTION PSYCHOLOGY:
HOW TO REMAIN CALM
WHILE THE SHARKS FEED

It will only be a matter of time before you buy a baseball card, set, or piece of memorabilia at a public auction. In more conventional markets—fine art, antiques, classic automobiles, for example—there is usually only one type of public bidding structure, the live, in-person auction. But the baseball market, alas, is not conventional. In fact, it's quite unconventional.

There are basically three kinds of baseball auctions. First, there's the live, in-person. Second, there's mail bid only. And third, there are telephone-bid auctions. Of course, everyone's auction rules are different, and you'll frequently notice a combination of some of the above. Phone bidders (and sometimes mail bidders) can usually bid at in-person auctions, and some mail-bid auctions accept phone bids during a time period just before bidding is closed.

The cost of bidding at auction is borne by the buyer, the seller, or a combination of the two. In some auctions, the house collects 10 percent from the winning bidder. In others, it takes 10 percent from the consignor only. Probably the fairest way to conduct an auction is to collect 5 percent each from buyer and seller, but I don't know anybody who does this, because the bookkeeping chores are automatically doubled. Simple logic dictates that it's cheaper to buy at auctions where the consignor foots the commission. Conversely, it's better to sell your goods at auctions where only the buyer pays. However, it's important to trust the auctioneer you're dealing with, and don't let the 10 percent become too big a factor. It's a small price to pay for comfort and quality.

Some auctions have minimum bids, others do not. Some require each bid to be advanced by 5 percent or 10 percent. Some simply advance bids at the discretion of the auctioneer. Some mail-bid auctions have special bidding features, such as "top all bids," meaning the house bids for you until you win with no preset limit. (You might want to find out what happens when two collectors want to put a top-all-bid order on the same lot. Usually they're both good clients, and the house has to take the first bid it received. But then, if they tell this to the one they don't take, isn't there some manipulation of the sale? Wouldn't knowing and disseminating the information that you're up against a top-all-bid buyer somehow be unfair? I think so.)

Some houses list presale estimates, others give them only when asked, and still others leave you completely in the dark—no advice at all. Some have liberal return policies, others have none. Some mail-bid auctions require deposits for certain high-estimate items.

Some cities have laws that compel auction houses to disclose certain information to the public. In New York City, the Department of Consumer Affairs requires that auctioneers must say when an item was "bought in"—meaning it failed to reach its reserve bid. The reserve bid is the minimum amount the consignor will settle for. Following the auction the house is required to furnish the gavel price to anyone who requests it. Operators of phone auctions, however, are not required to disclose prices.

You also must consider the total cost of goods by including sales tax (unless you have a state resale number) in a winning bid. For instance, it can be quite expensive to bid at auction in

New York City. Say you buy something for $750. With a 10 percent commission, the winning bid is now $825. Including city and state sales tax of 8.25 percent, you pay $893.06, a 19 percent premium over the hammer price.

If all this sounds intimidating, it is. But don't fret. Your first rule is not to bid at any auction you don't feel comfortable with. I don't recommend bidding by mail or phone on any item, no matter how routine (like a $40 Hank Aaron baseball), if it isn't pictured in the catalog or the advertisement. It's just impossible to tell what the condition is. Sometimes, even with the photo (usually on newsprint, or in a catalog printed on good paper), you cannot always tell the condition, anyway. But any kind of reproduction usually makes an item look worse, with the possible exception of a baseball. Remember, they all look "white" when printed on white stock. So if you like what you see in the photo, then you'll probably like the item a little better when you see it in the flesh. Caution: Shellacked baseballs are usually *not* noticeable in photos.

Be wary of items that are not fully pictured, such as a baseball with multiple signatures. Smart auction holders will usually photograph the objects with the best side to the camera. So if the HOF or star signatures mentioned in the blurb aren't visible (but the common player autographs are), then you can be sure that the unseen autographs are in poor or barely readable shape. Of course, if you're bidding with an auction holder who is reliable and forthright, then the item's condition will be honestly and meticulously disclosed.

But still you must be very careful when you read the descriptive blurbs. Remember, they are the auctioneer's only sales tools, so he's trying to be informative, but he also wants to be vague enough to hide flaws and still hype an item enough to bring a high price. Let me show you what I mean. Let's say a catalog lists the following baseball cards (these are actual listings):

1960 Topps #1 Early Wynn, well centered, sharp, Mint (no photo)...$50–60.

1960 Topps #200 Willie Mays, bright and fresh, Mint
(no photo)..$125–150.

At the time the catalog was printed, the price guides listed
the Wynn card at $35 and the Mays at $100 in near mint
condition. What should you assume about the centering of the
cards in the ad? One is "well centered," and the centering in
the other is not described at all. Both are estimated at well over
the near mint price guide quote. Should it be 50-50, or 60-40, or
even 70-30? You don't know, and neither do I. They may be
great cards, but if you want to bid on them badly enough, it's
worth a long-distance call to find out.

MR. MINT'S MAXIM: *Do not bid on anything that
has the notation "no photo" unless you received a
detailed description of the item's condition. I especially advise against bidding on cards by phone
unless their condition is meticulously described.*

The very best auction you can patronize is one you can
attend. There are three important reasons. One, you can
personally inspect and usually handle the items in advance.
Two, you can make a calculated judgment on whether an item
will attract a flurry of interest or little at all. And three, and
perhaps most important, you can see who is bidding against
you.

When you go to an auction, arrive very early. Then take your
catalog and make a random check of the condition of some of
the items. Make detailed notes in your catalog of the condition
of anything you're seriously interested in, especially if it's not
thoroughly described. If you see a card, for example, that has a
surprisingly low estimate in terms of the current market, then

the condition should be the reason. An EX-MT Nolan Ryan rookie card will have $850–$950 instead of the NR MT to MT $1,250 to $1,500. Remember, this is a good time to ask auction personnel to see supporting documentation. Letters of authenticity *increase* an item's value. Why? Because so many collectibles in the business exchange hands without letters of authenticity.

Plan to sit somewhere near the middle of the room, or at least far enough back where you won't have to crane your neck to see who's bidding. When you find yourself seated at your rookie auction, my advice is to leave your paddle in your lap, despite your burning desire to come home with something. (In fact, to be really conservative, don't even register for a bidding number. Just watch and make notes.) It will feel a lot like being set loose on a shopping spree and being told you can't buy anything, but as a first-time bidder you will be up against knowledgeable collectors and longtime dealers. Their experience gives them an instinct on what's overvalued or undervalued. They have a huge edge, and you shouldn't bid on anything until you're relaxed enough to know your pulse won't be wildly careening through your carotid artery.

There is a reason that the bidder gets a paddle and the auctioneer is the only one who quotes the current price. The psychology here is to remove as much as possible the feeling that you're spending hard cash to buy something. This is the same logic that a gambling casino uses. Notice how quickly cash disappears and is replaced by chips. When you are in a gambling casino atmosphere long enough, you begin to ever so slightly lose the association between a chip and the currency it represents. Of course, you never totally forget you're gambling with real money, but you're much more willing to get involved in the action. Whoever dreamed up the idea of using chips was a genius, and so, too, was the man who conjured up the numbered auction paddle. It's faster, more convenient, and less cumbersome to raise a paddle than it is to shout "Four hundred!"

Understand that the order of the lots, or the pacing of the

product, is carefully thought out well in advance by the auction house. The auctioneer is putting up the lots in the order that he thinks will generate the most income and, hence, the biggest commissions. Most good houses put a few marquee lots on the block early, because that's when the collective bankroll in the room is at its fattest. If it's a rare, very expensive item, he'll probably know in advance who'll be in the hunt. He also must be smart enough to save a few choice items for the end, because he doesn't want to watch the room empty too soon before the last object is gaveled down.

What advantages over the guy sitting next to you can you glean from the preceding analysis?

The better buys may emerge when the bidding rush dies, which is soon after the top lots have been sold. After a particularly expensive lot is gaveled down, the room is often just catching its breath. While everyone is inhaling, marveling at how much someone just shelled out for a given antique, there's often disinterest in the next few lots. Perhaps the best bargains will reveal themselves in the last third of the auction, especially if there are many lots offered. In September 1990, Richard Wolffers Auctions, Inc., a San Francisco–based auctioneer, held an auction with 1,056 lots. An elaborate, well-illustrated catalog was offered a month before the sale, and mail bidding was provided for those who could not attend. Luck, as well as stamina, was required to find a good buy.

It's difficult to maintain your concentration for five or six hours at a time, so it's better to pick out a block of 20 or 30 lots and focus on those. If there's a lot that interests you outside that block, you can ask a friend to bid for you or leave a written bid. It's an added expense to hire a dealer or professional agent to bid at auction, but well-heeled collectors often do this. The reasons are (a) they're too busy to attend, (b) they prefer anonymity, and (c) they're paying for the dealer's appraisal—he will tell his client what he thinks an item will sell for and advise him on what should be his bidding limit. Dealers or agents usually tack on an extra 10 percent of the hammer price for their trouble. Though it sounds like something you'll never need, it is not a bad idea if you're thinking of someday buying a piece of baseball memorabilia at auction in the $10,000 to $20,000 price range.

Obviously, luck will favor the better-prepared bidders. Those include potential buyers who know the rarity, condition, and market range of every item they're bidding on. They know how often the exact items (or similar ones) they're interested in have come up on the block, and they've noted what the gavel price was. In fact, it's important to keep all the recent catalogs (within one to two years) with the prices carefully filled out. Auctions are conducted so quickly that it's impossible to do any research in the heat of bidding.

Smart bidders also have contingency plans, as well as strict budgets, either for each item or for a number of lots together. They're disciplined, just like a savvy dealer. They don't lose their cool when the bidding is brisk. Be the best-prepared bidder in the room. Know what your budget is. Don't overextend yourself, and above all, focus on a few choice lots. It's better to confine your attention to the more expensive lots than several cheap ones. Don't feel defeated if you come away with nothing, even after you've actively bid on several items. Let the other guy overpay. There will always be another auction. There will always be another lot.

MR. MINT'S MAXIM: *Most of the time it is preferable to enter the bidding toward the end, when you believe the action on a particular lot is slowing down.*

On the other hand, if there is considerable interest in a lot—something you can often discern before the bidding begins—it might pay to make a large, preemptive bid immediately, without waiting for the auctioneer to step it up. This has great shock value, and also has the effect of shutting out a lot of potential bidders. Of course, it can backfire, too. You could end up owning something after a single bid and woefully overpaying for it. If an item is listed for $150–$200 in the catalog, and you're fairly certain it will not be purchased for less than $250, it might be worth instantly blurting what you think might be the high bid. Just make sure it's not any higher than you normally would have bid, anyway.

There is a certain amount of truth in the adage, "Know thine enemy," and it's particularly apt at an auction. Most live auctions are about two-thirds dealers and one-third collectors, so you'll often find yourself up against someone who buys and sells this material for his livelihood. At large, professional auction galleries that deal in all kinds of goods—Christie's in New York City, for example—the ratio is more like two-thirds collectors versus one-third dealers. Baseball card dealers will stay away when they're reasonably certain that everything will go for very high prices.

But dealers face the same problems as collectors and amateur speculators, because they're often bidding against each other. A few years ago, when the Cleveland Sports Museum auctioned off its collection, I found myself going head-to-head against Pat Quinn, another dealer, for all the very rare Shoeless Joe Jackson memorabilia. He went home with some of it, and I went home with some. But the bottom line was that we both overpaid for several items, because we were locked in a constant bidding duel.

MR. MINT'S MAXIM: *There are times when you'll be bidding against a dealer or collector with unshakable resolve. He'll hold his paddle up with a casual, arrogant air, and he'll bury his nose in his catalog. He is telling the room he won't retreat at any price. Let someone else bid against him.*

It's critically important to scout the room and learn who are the dealers, and who are the ardent collectors with deep pockets who won't think twice about overpaying for a lot simply because they must own it. If you're shy, you'll have to become a bit more gregarious than usual. While you're waiting for the auction to get under way, you might strike up a chat with the gentleman next to you. Everyone else is slightly nervous, too, and if he's a veteran, he'll probably gab a bit. Perhaps you can cajole him into discreetly identifying some of the room's heavy hitters. After a few auctions, you'll begin to notice them on your own.

MR. MINT'S MAXIM: *Many collectors are terrified of going head-on with a dealer at an auction. This is fallacious thinking, especially if it's only you against a single dealer. Remember, the dealer most likely has a client to whom he's planning to resell the piece. Obviously, he expects to make a profit. So he's hoping to pay, at most, slightly less than retail. The moment to worry about overpaying for a lot is when all the active bidders who are dealers have dropped their paddles for good.*

The new reality of auctions, both with baseball cards and with any other collectibles, is that their popularity has caused almost everything to be sold for retail or *higher*. The days of wholesale bargains are long gone, because the bidding audience in general is too knowledgeable to let anyone steal anything. There are too many collectors in the audience who assume it will cost more next week, especially if they are forced to buy it from a dealer who just made the winning bid. So, remember, everyone in the room is bidding into a bull market, though not everybody is willing to admit it.

Buyer's remorse is a feeling that everyone experiences at one time or another when he is a winning bidder. The best way to overcome it is to know that if you had doubts about going so high, somebody had to be the underbidder. If you're gaveled down at $1,500 on an item that was estimated at $1,000 to $1,200, take some comfort in knowing that someone else bid $1,400. Conversely, you will sometimes be the underbidder and find yourself undergoing "should have bought it" remorse. This is one subjunctive mood you can overcome by realizing that the other guy most likely wouldn't let you have it for one more final bid. You bid $800, he says $850. You leave thinking you could have had it for $900. But what if he says $950? Now you're back to where you were $100 ago. The first time you hesitate should be your last.

It's probably unfortunate, but the auction trend has moved in past years toward mail and phone bidding. The problem is, of course, geography. The business moves so quickly, and it's so difficult to get collectors from all over the nation under one roof on a single evening that it's become necessary to make other arrangements. I hold six major telephone auctions a year, every two months, where I sell around 200 high-quality items. Bidders must register in advance and are assigned a bidding number. I charge 10 percent to the consignor only. I run a photo of every item I sell.

If you're going to bid on one of the dozen or so mail or phone auctions listed each week in SCD, you must be careful to read the auction rules. I run a full-page ad explaining what mine are, so I'd recommend passing on any auctions that don't clearly disclose its rules. (Every week SCD runs a 13-point "Usual Mail Bid Rules" column next to its advertising index. Most reputable auction holders follow them.)

If you're mailing in bids from a catalog or ad, I'd recommend sending them by certified mail, return receipt requested, especially if the lots you're bidding on are fairly expensive. This way there can be no dispute over a bid "not received." Or you can call the auctioneer to confirm if he's received your bids.

There are a number of phone-only auctions offered all the time, and many are listed in the "Baseball Card Phone Shoppers Quality Item Auction," which is a consortium of dealers that changes on a weekly basis. There appears to be a lot of good stuff offered, but only a handful of items are pictured, and there is no phone number for further inquiries. I find it impossible to recommend, especially since the bidding phone number is always a "900" number. This means bidders are charged $2 for the first minute and $1 for each additional minute per call. To know where you stand on any given lot, you'll have to make a lot of expensive calls. Why should you have to pay more than the cost of a conventional toll call to bid? It's ridiculous, and I'd be hard-pressed advising you to bid at any 900-number auction.

The other big problem with phone-only auctions is the bid-closing rules. Many say that the auction closes after the phone stops ringing for five or ten minutes, or some other arbitrary time period. Some have a time deadline, which causes bidders to become frantic when their calls are met with constant busy signals during the final hour. Obviously, bidding on these is often a confused hassle. I wouldn't stay up until the wee hours worrying about whether I'd get a bid in. Remember, there's much rampant speculation in the business. Items that come up at auction often resurface again at the next one.

This last piece of advice on auctions is especially useful when the industry goes through a minor dip or strong recession. Sometimes consignors have very high hopes on their lots, and set unrealistically large reserves. Auctioneers sometimes won't even ask sellers to lower their expectations, because they need as much good material as possible to attract a crowd of bidders. When there are a number of buy-ins, put a "B.I." notation in your catalog, especially on lots you might have second thoughts on. If a lot is estimated at $600 to $700, the reserve may be at $550. Suppose the final bid was only $500, and you're beginning to think it might have been a good buy.

When the auction is over, leave your name and number with

the auctioneer. Tell him that you're interested in cutting a deal for a certain unsold lot, perhaps for the reserve price—if it's realistic—with the seller. He'll usually make another overture—he wants to make the sale. Remember, the auctioneer is still entitled to his commission (he often charges the seller a small fee for unsold goods, anyway), so be clear in advance that you're willing to pay it.

Above all, when you have that paddle in your lap: patience and prudence.

AUTHENTICITY PRIMER:
HOW TO SPOT COUNTERFEITS

On more than one occasion I've heard the following story. At a card show, a reputable dealer strolls up to the table of another reputable dealer, albeit one who normally does a more modest volume of business. The strolling dealer perhaps has a serious collector in tow, and the first thing he does is begin inspecting the expensive auto-graphed balls at the table. After careful perusal, the strolling dealer blurts out that the balls the guy is selling are all fake. The dealer at the table calmly replies, "Well, Mr. ____, then I'm sure you can explain everything to a judge, because I bought them from you last year."

If you are around this business long enough, you will see everything. In the early 1980s, a California businessman was convicted of counterfeiting the 1963 Topps Pete Rose rookie card. He spent two days in jail and was fined $1,000. He had about 12,000 cards, and when he was nailed, the court ordered the cards destroyed. The shredding machine broke down, and when the guy found out about it, his lawyer arranged for the remaining cards to be spared so long as they were stamped "counterfeit" on the reverse. You can probably guess what happened. The guy began selling the fakes for a few bucks apiece. They're now collectibles, and the price has gone up to more than $20 a card.

The person who uttered the phrase about how crime doesn't pay obviously wasn't as industrious as this gentleman.

Prior to the 1980s, the baseball card and collectible hobby was virtually free of fraud. Then in 1982 or 1983, the hobby's spectacular growth saw numerous cases of outright deception, phony antiques made overnight. It's certainly a poor reflection on the industry that this chapter is even necessary. But most dealers, those who value treating their clients honestly, rationalize the problem by noting there's always a small percentage in every profession who spoil it for everyone else. Car dealer, coin dealer, flea marketer, whoever.

When you finish this chapter, you'll have a reasonably good idea of how crooks attempt to place phonies into the marketplace. Illegal reproductions range from crude and easily recognizable to very slick—slick enough to fool many unsuspecting dealers.

In 1989, the *Philadelphia Inquirer* published a four-part exposé about the business entitled, "From a Kids' Pastime to a Field of Greed." The articles detailed several instances of misconduct, from mail fraud to forged autographs to all kinds of schemes perpetuated by con men from coast to coast. Many people in the business criticized the series as being too polemical, too one-sided. But this kind of jolt, amid all the great stories about how cards have become big business and terrific investments, was inevitable and probably necessary. For new collectors, it provided an invaluable service. The message was clear: Maintain a healthy skepticism, especially if a deal looks too good to be true.

Paul Sumner, a former printer and a baseball enthusiast, actually got the idea to start manufacturing the very high-quality Upper Deck cards after he spotted a bunch of suspicious 1984 Donruss Don Mattingly cards in a hobby store. The cards just didn't look or feel right. He explained to the dealer—who had just bought 100 of them at an incredibly low price—that the printing was light, there were smudges, and the cardboard even had a different texture to it.

As I explained earlier, Upper Deck's cards are printed on superior stock and have holograms to deter counterfeiting. The packs are sealed at the factory in tamper-resistant tinfoil. Sumner went one step further than the other card companies. He made sure that every pack was randomly mixed. From past experience, he knew that many dealers could figure out the mixing patterns of various companies. For instance, it was discovered that in the 1989 Topps packs, you would always find the Will Clark card between Luis Polonia and Bob Walk. In the Fleer issue of that season, Clark was sandwiched in between Mike Moore and Paul Gibson.

Why do dealers make such a point of learning the sequence? Well, for one, the young collectors do it, and there had to be some 12-year-old kid who first began sorting through cellophane packs and rack packs (multiple cellos) to find out who was in between the players featured on the front and back. If you found a Bobby Heisel and the Milwaukee Brewers team card on the ends of a 1975 Topps rack pack, you knew you were going to get the Yount and Brett rookie cards, which are close in numerical order in that series. Anybody who knew this bought those rack packs whenever they could. There were a lot of them around many years ago, but now, of course, they've disappeared. Those packs only had a greater perceived value to those in the know back in the early 1980s, when Brett and Yount rookie cards began to increase in value (after all, they weren't worth very much when they were first printed).

Knowing this kind of thing requires research. It's not illegal, and it's not deceptive as long as nobody cheats anybody or tampers with packs.

Pack tampering is a despicable practice, and unfortunately it does occur. How common is it? Nobody knows. Tampering can often occur on wax, cellophane, or rack packs, because un-opened material has taken on a great investment premium.

Dealers and collectors often wonder about Donruss rack packs. For some reason they aren't always sealed very tightly, and it makes tampering tempting to the unscrupulous. A guy who is handy with a scalpel can take a mint 1984 Donruss Mattingly card and slip it onto the top or bottom of an ordinary rack pack. Just by slitting it, he now has turned a $100 pack into one worth $400 to $500.

MR. MINT'S MAXIM: *You will continually come across advertising that says "Guaranteed Unsearched" or "Guaranteed Unopened." It may mean absolutely nothing. Why are those guarantees necessary? Because of the hobby's general level of suspicion. You must really know and trust whom you're buying from if you're going to buy unopened material. The older the unopened material, the more careful you should be.*

Inspect the back of a 1991 wax pack of any brand other than Upper Deck. You'll notice the way it is folded, and you'll also see that it is seldom sealed all the way across the back. If it's very tightly sealed, there's an excellent chance that it's an "iron job." That's when an unscrupulous dealer uses a hot iron to reseal rare wax packs that he's searched for rookie or star cards. Usually, when he closes them, he makes the mistake of making sure the entire middle fold is sealed. (The practice of removing star and rookie cards from packs and replacing them with worthless common cards is known as "cherry picking.") Occasionally, you'll see packs resealed with Vaseline. Sometimes tampered packs show a little bit of the wax cracking, in the corners of the pack or where the other folds are. Cello and rack packs are just as easy to open and reseal. A rack pack can be slit open with a razor blade in the cellophane separating the packs and then resealed with clear glue.

Perhaps the most common type of fraud among cards occurs when the corners of a legitimate card are microscopically trimmed with a razor blade or X-Acto knife. This practice is often attempted with old cards in very good to excellent condition. Usually, these cards have one or two slightly soft or worn corners, where if there hadn't been such a flaw, their condition would easily move up a grade. Trimming is also done to turn an off-centered card into a well-centered one. With cards like Batter Ups, Cracker Jacks, Goudeys, Allen & Ginters, Turkey Reds, or the T-205 and T-206 series, altering the corners can generate thousands of dollars. A few years ago, a guy was caught with a bunch of trimmed T-206 cards trying to sell them at a major convention.

It's easy to tell if a card has been trimmed. All you need is a small ruler, and a price guide that publishes a card's manufactured dimensions. Let's say you find a 1914 Cracker Jack Walter Johnson card, which easily sells for four figures in excellent to mint condition. You want to buy the card because it looks really wonderful, and it has four sharp corners. You've done your homework, and you know that the Cracker Jacks are supposed to measure 2¼ by 3 inches. You ask the dealer if he minds if you measure the card—it's not an uncommon request on high-cost items. In fact, if he's confident it's been unaltered, he will welcome your diligence. If the card measures 2³⁄₁₆ by 2¹⁵⁄₁₆ inches, you'll know that it's no good.

A sixteenth of an inch, or even less, can be a long distance in this business. It can also mean financial disaster.

I'm surprised how many collectors don't bother measuring expensive cards. Several years ago, I tried marketing a low-cost plastic measuring tool, one a hobbyist could carry in his pocket to shows. I sold very few, even though it was priced at $4.95 and I'd be making only a modest profit. My aim was to help educate the collecting public. Apparently, most people are forever trustful. But if you're going to be buying high-ticket items, you want to be sure you haven't been taken by a doctored card.

There are two other, more minor problems associated with bad baseball cards. One is the unidentified or poorly labeled reproduction. The major companies have made available low-cost reprints of many of the legendary, tough-to-find series of cards. These cards are prominently labeled on either the front or the reverse as reprints and are harmless. If you see an old card that appears to be too new, just make sure you look for the reproduction designation. Only rarely will an optimistic crook try to pass one of these off as real, but it does happen, so you should be aware of it. Sometimes a crafty dealer will show you a reproduction card and wait to see how quickly you notice it's one. He doesn't mean to be purely deceptive; he's using it as a way of finding out what kind of experience you have.

Far more serious are the questionable ethics shrouding the professional restoration of old baseball cards. There is a fellow in the trade who once specialized in this, and other dealers and myself finally decided against having anything to do with these cards. The restorer had meticulously taken old Goudey cards and built up the corners, even to the extent that he used the same cardboard from other Goudeys. His work was something akin to a mechanic who restores old automobiles by scavenging parts from other junk cars.

There is nothing intrinsically wrong with a restored card, if it is clearly labeled "restored," just like a reprint card. But the guy had put only a small dot on the card, not to be misleading but to make the cards look as close to their original mint condition as possible. He never tried to fob them off as "original" mint condition cards. But here's the rub. Suppose you buy the card as restored, and then sell it as restored. The guy who buys it from you can resell it and say whatever he wants. You have no control over what happens to it once it's gone.

The restorer stopped doing this work, mainly because he found out he was allergic to the chemicals he was using. And everyone in the business is the better off because of it.

MR. MINT'S MAXIM: *If you're wondering whether a card has been restored and not identified as such, a simple inspection can be made. Hold the card up to a strong light. The corners will be slightly translucent.*

The autograph market is the area where perhaps the largest amount of fraud occurs. And it's obvious why. Famous signatures—especially those on the right items—command a lot of money now, and some are very easy to copy. I have one friend, a young dealer, who often sends me a "greeting card" at shows. One of those had the freshly written signatures of Babe Ruth, Mickey Mantle, and Pete Rose. The autographs, of course, came from his own hand, and he meant nothing malicious. But when I've showed them to other dealers, they're astonished— one even used the word "frightening"—by how real they look. Untrained eyes would be easily duped.

Fake signatures can and do pop up just about anywhere—on balls, bats, jerseys, and batting gloves—and it's worth studying the following list to get an idea of the more commonly bogus autographs that often appear at shows.

> Roger Maris
> Babe Ruth
> Joe DiMaggio
> Lou Gehrig
> Pete Rose
> Jackie Robinson
> Ty Cobb

There should be nothing surprising about those seven players. Their signatures are in great demand—Robinson, Cobb,

Ruth, and Gehrig are worth $3,000 and up on just about any item—and their handwriting is not particularly difficult to duplicate, especially by counterfeiters who have made thousands of practice runs. Phony DiMaggio balls are apparently very common. I know of one collector who'd love to own a single-signed DiMaggio ball, but he hasn't seen one he trusts. The only one he'll buy is one where he witnesses DiMag himself signing it. Since he's not signing balls anymore, this collector admits he'll probably never buy one. That's a shame, but that's the way it is.

Sports Collectors Digest has published the *Baseball Autograph Handbook,* which includes several signature specimens of every member of the Hall of Fame. It's somewhat useful but not totally reliable, since I've already bumped into a sports autograph expert who maintains that several signatures used in the book as genuine are, in fact, suspect. Such a book is necessary, however, and it points out that many older players who've signed their names over many years have sometimes experienced dramatic changes in their handwriting. There's nothing unusual about someone's signature changing, especially if they begin signing hundreds of times in a day at a card show. Even an experienced bank teller knows that no two signatures are exactly alike. But there are certain stylistic things that remain constant, the small "e" in Ruth's autograph, and the capital "J" in DiMaggio's.

There is another theory attached to counterfeit autographs that you should not put much faith in. That's the one that follows the argument that a guy printing bogus money doesn't bother with fives or tens, because it doesn't pay. The bills most commonly counterfeited are twenties, fifties, and hundreds. The autographs of players like Nolan Ryan, Bench, Mantle, Canseco, and Bo Jackson are in great supply, because these guys sign all the time. Relative to tough autographs, they're fairly inexpensive. Because the supply is so great, counterfeiters have little fear that the market can become any more saturated than it already is. Also, they think, "Who's going to question the authenticity of a Bench autograph when you can buy one for $20?"

MR. MINT'S MAXIM: *Buy autographed items only from reliable dealers who can offer some guarantee of origination or authenticity. For example, when I paid Reggie Jackson to sign bats, I had my picture taken with him at the signing session. On high-priced items, insist on a letter of authenticity signed by the player, or his agent or lawyer.*

The "ghost signature" has become an ugly occurrence, largely because of the huge demands made on players by the new hordes of collectors. It's nothing new. Some baseball autograph experts have speculated that more than a few of the famous players of the early days of baseball frequently had clubhouse personnel or batboys pinch-hit for them on 8″ by 10″ publicity stills or baseballs. In a way, you can't blame them. Popular stars are asked to sign so much nowadays that some collectors feel it's the player's obligation and their right to have it. When Johnny Bench played, he used a rubber stamp when deluged by mail requests sent to the clubhouse. Bench didn't mean any harm, and he also didn't worry about insulting the serious autograph hound.

Probably the greatest mystery surrounding a ghost signature is the infamous case of Shoeless Joe Jackson. Any casual student of baseball lore knows that Joe Jackson has the third highest batting average of all time, and was one of those involved in the Black Sox scandal and barred for life from baseball. Jackson was a mill hand from South Carolina who was functionally illiterate. Since he could neither read his own contracts nor write his own name, most serious historians think that any "Joe Jackson" signature is spurious at best. Some say Jackson could sign only his own name and write nothing else; others say that an "X" was all he could manage. The SCD once published a facsimile of his driver's license, but that does little to counter the very cogent argument that his wife handled all his paperwork, including signing his name. It makes a good deal of sense that Mrs. Jackson was his one and only ghost signer.

One cannot make a Joe Jackson autograph real merely by wishing it so, any more than one can hope any forgery is genuine. My advice here is give up the ghost of Joe Jackson's autograph. Nobody can say for certain whether it's real.

Roy Campanella is one player whose autograph has two different versions. The first kind are precious and few, and had to have been executed prior to his crippling automobile accident in 1957. Far more common are Campy's glove-aided signatures (and rubber-stamp facsimiles, typically used for the legions of mail requests). Campanella has full use of his arm but no control over his hand. A few years ago a collector invented a glove that specially holds a pen, so he can sign, but the results are not as nice as his beautiful and lyrical handwriting specimens from before the accident. Campanella has appeared occasionally at autograph shows; in one instance I noted a promoter charging $225 per signature with a strict limit of 450. There is no reason for it to be worth as much as one of his autographs signed more than three decades ago. Considering that his pre-accident signature costs five times as much or more, the glove-aided autograph is a relative bargain.

MR. MINT'S MAXIM: *Keep a vigilant eye peeled to the quality of the autographs on old, multi-signature baseballs. A good rule of thumb is that the fading over the years should be relatively uniform, especially on balls where the players are all deceased and there was a strong likelihood they signed at the same time, or during the same season. I would be especially wary of a ball that had one or two signatures that were darker (the stars or HOFers)* *than the others. Some very naive collectors have copied over autographs in an effort to darken what has become almost unreadable. This, of course, can make a ball virtually worthless. If you see a very dark signature, be suspicious.*

If you're about to invest a lot of money in a very expensive autographed item, it's always wise to have the ball independently appraised. If the autograph experts are not in concurrence about a signature's validity (and this has happened many times), I would go so far as having an ink test performed by somebody completely removed from the business. There are a number of these firms, which charge $100 to $250, for a test. A good test will be able to pinpoint within a fairly narrow period when the signature was written.

Know the basics of the modern writing instruments. The blue and black Sharpie felt-tip pens are the preferred autograph pens for photos and other flat items. One particularly popular model was first made by the Sanford Corp. of Bellwood, Illinois, in 1977. So if someone is trying to sell you a Goose Goslin autographed signed in "beautiful Sharpie," you should kindly remind him that Goslin died in 1971, and that the odds of his resurrection are greatly against him.

I cannot emphasize enough the deception problems wrought by the popularity of game-worn jerseys, caps, and bats. I've touched on some of this in the chapters on memorabilia collecting. There are two important additional hints I'd like to share, however. First, whenever a player incurs financial problems (from either poor management or bad investments), his memorabilia—lots of it—suddenly begins appearing at shows. Gaylord Perry and Pete Rose are two examples. Perry was said to have changed jerseys and caps during his 300th win, and everyone already knows about Rose's shenanigans. It's not enough to read the hobby trades. Stay current with the nation's sports pages, because players' financial problems (as well as every tiny indiscretion) are often made public.

Second, sometimes you must question not just the item, but the attesting documentation. Letters of authenticity can easily be manufactured. Steve Carlton's last jersey (he was released by the Minnesota Twins in 1988) appeared at a show. The clubhouse attendant who actually sent Carlton's last uniform back to the Twins minor-league affiliate was baffled, even with the attesting letter. Carlton later disavowed the uniform's authenticity, but some dealer or collector may still be hoping it's real.

INVESTMENT STRATEGIES FOR THE 1990s: BULL DURHAMS AND BAD NEWS BEARS

So far, I've acquainted you with much general advice, offered caution, and deluged you with several rules of thumb regarding collecting and investing. Now I'd like to address some of the specific economic issues surrounding investing in baseball cards and collectibles. Are baseball cards and memorabilia subject to the same vicissitudes that affect the prices of other collectibles and antiques? It's difficult to say. So far, I think not. It's tough to imagine how the 1990 Iraqi invasion of Kuwait affected the price of an old or rare baseball card.

Are baseball cards recession-proof? No. Nothing is recession-proof, in my opinion. Baseball cards are recession-*resistant*. There was a soft spot in the 1981 market, but it is not the same as the one we began experiencing in the 1990 season while this book was being prepared. The 1981 recession was to some extent related to a general economic downturn, but it was mainly due to the emergence of the hobby as a full-fledged business. Remember, the baseball card market was not born fully formed.

In 1981, thanks to the first barrage of publicity, thousands of Mickey Mantle cards came out of the attics. You couldn't sell them all. There was too much product, and there was a subsequent lowering of prices, even though the demand was strong. But as more people came into the business, the prices steadily rose again. There is no sign of a long-term bear market. More likely, there will be short periods of stagnation, where buying and selling volume decreases, like slow trading of the Dow Jones Industrials.

If an analyst plotted the card prices from 1980 to 1990, you would see a dip in 1981, and the remainder of the chart lines pointing upward at various angles. The important thing to remember is that two factors affect the market's general index: old cards and newer cards which include still-active players.

Old-card prices are more driven by the bigger economic factors that drive any commodity, while new cards are driven by what kind of season a player had. The first factor may be somewhat predictable, while the second is more often unpredictable. More specifically, what kind of an effect does the acute movement upward of a Kevin Maas 1990 rookie card have on the Cobbs, Ruths, and Gehrigs? It's almost impossible to tell. How much does general inflation artificially boost the price (and consequently reduce the value) of cards? Real monetary growth must factor the negative effect of inflation in its equation, because money has less value or purchasing power as time marches on.

There probably isn't a financial expert astute enough to sort it out. (If he existed, he should be solving the nation's trillion-dollar-debt problem.) This is why if you're considering investing large amounts in cards, a dealer who professes enough expertise to "manage your portfolio" will be no better than the average broker at Shearson Lehman Hutton. He'll merely say cards have gone up between 20 and 35 percent a year, and though he might not be wrong, he hasn't told you exactly how the losing investments and unrealistic increases in lucky cards has affected the overall general price index. (He'll say, "What is Rosen talking about? There is no general price index." He's right, but that's my point.)

Every free market has its touts and prognosticators, its

expert analysts, and this market is no different. You'll find "investment" newsletters in every phase of the business. Some are good, some are not so hot. A number of investors have made many successful calls, and, of course, some have had their share of dogs. As with any Wall Street analyst, nobody's right all the time, and it takes an honest seer to publicly admit his mistakes (such as I've detailed earlier).

But in this chapter I'm obliged to crawl slowly out on the proverbial limb. Aside from the prudence I've preached in previous chapters, I'm going to predict which cards and items have the best growth potential in this decade, and I'm also going to take my best swing at telling you which investments will be overrated.

Here is a handful of suggestions, in no particular order, where I think there will be long-term growth. Investors some-times should expect to pay higher than book value for top-condition material but it shouldn't matter. In terms of yearly appreciation, the following will be excellent buys.

1. Any cards or items (especially one-of-a-kind collectibles) from the nineteenth century. So little material (relatively speaking) from baseball's early years has survived in good condition that the best stuff is certain to keep climbing.

2. Adrian C. "Cap" Anson and Larry "Napoleon" Lajoie. Of all the old-timers, these two players carry the most demand and mystique. Anson played entirely in the nineteenth century, while Lajoie began his career in the 1890s and played through the teens. The 1887 N28 Allen & Ginter #1 Anson is a sight to behold. The first card of the first tobacco series, Cap is shown contemplatively holding his bat, handlebar mustache perfectly waxed. A near mint card was listed in an auction catalog in 1990 at $1,500 to $1,750. It's easily worth $2,000.

3. The 1919 Black Sox players: Chick Gandil, Ed Cicotte, Lefty Williams, Buck Weaver, Happy Felsch, Swede Risberg, Fred McMullin, and primarily, Joe Jackson. It's a rare event when a World Series is fixed, and the public fascination with this scandal never ebbs. Some dealers felt that the movie *Eight Men Out* boosted the prices of Black Sox material, but I don't agree. People who saw the movie weren't collectors, and those collectors interested in the 1919 team already knew more than the movie revealed, because they had read Eliot Asinof's classic 1963 book about it.

4. Any items from the Negro leagues. The most popular players were Satchel Paige, Judy Johnson, Cool Papa Bell, and Josh Gibson, all HOFers. (Dandridge, DiHigo, Leonard, Irvin, and Lloyd were also elected to the HOF, though Irvin is better known for his eight major-league seasons.) Posters, pennants, scorecards are all in big demand, and this is enhanced by the inclusion of any of the HOFers. I predict a steady, strong increase in these items.

A few black stars who played in the major leagues also did stints in the Negro leagues. Ernie Banks, Jackie Robinson, and Elston Howard spent part of their careers with the Kansas City Monarchs. Minnie Minoso, Larry Doby, Roy Campanella, and Jim Gilliam played for all-black teams. And how many fans know that Willie Mays played three seasons with the Black Barons?

5. A 1969 Topps set of cards in near mint to mint condition. This is one of those sets that are "condition scarce." It's commonly available in excellent condition, but very few top-quality ones come on the market. Another reason is that the printing and centering are uneven on many star cards. The Reggie Jackson and the two "white" and "yellow" lettered Mantles (500A and 500B) constitute half the set's value, so make sure those cards are elegant. The 1969s also contain Ryan's and Bench's second-year cards and Seaver's third-year card.

6. A 1958 Topps set in near mint to mint condition, especially the difficult first series (1–110). These are extremely difficult to find (at least I never see any).

7. A 1954 Topps set in near mint to mint condition. This set contains the rookie cards of Aaron, Banks, and Kaline (but no Mantle, because he appeared exclusively on the Bowman's that season).

8. The 1914 Cracker Jack set of 144 cards. This is a very beautiful and expensive set of cards (it has red backgrounds) featured as prizes in the Cracker Jack boxes. In 1987, baseball card writer Frank Slocum mentioned in a book that a full set was worth around $9,000. The 1990 Beckett's featured the set at $27,000 in excellent to mint condition. This is a 205 percent appreciation in three years, or approximately 70 percent per annum. I don't think it will get any cheaper, though investors will probably have to settle for somewhat smaller annual increases.

9. Any star cards (in near mint or better condition) from the 1911 T-205 (gold border) and 1909-11 T-206 (white border) tobacco series. These are very expensive per-card investments, but they're so prized by collectors, good cards are always in demand and are easily liquidated. I'm also high on any of the cards—commons or stars—in the oversized T-3 Turkey Reds. The complete set has doubled in price in the three years from 1987 to 1990.

10. The two sets the Goudey Gum Company issued in 1933 and 1934. These were known as bubble gum cards, 20 years before Topps borrowed the idea. The 1933 set contains the elusive Nap Lajoie card (#106), which the company inadvertently left out of the set and didn't get around to printing until the following year. Even then, it was issued in limited numbers and only sent to collectors who specifically requested it. Lajoie's card is perhaps the most coveted baseball card after the Honus Wagner T-206.

11. Unopened material, especially pre-1980 cards. I'm a bullish fan of unopened cards, because as long as they stay unopened, nobody argues about the condition. Unopened wax packs have an indefinable quality—maybe because they're tactile and they feel old?—and they escalate in price very quickly, because they're becoming increasingly difficult to find. Boxes and cases are also desirable, but you must be very acquainted with current availability and price fluctuation, because the trading is widespread and brisk.

In a five-month period between January and May in 1990, I bought several 1952 Topps wax packs at $300 (and quickly resold them for $500). They were then auctioned at more than $1,000 apiece, and appeared for sale in May at shows for $1,400 to $2,000.

Since I'm most frequently asked about investing in Topps issues (1952 to 1991), here are my specific evaluations of some cards and sets.

The 1952 Topps issue, the company's first full year, is considered the premier complete set of the postwar period. (Topps actually issued 134 cards in three sets—the "reds," "blues," and "current All-Stars"—and a "team" set in 1951, but they're fairly rare.) The 1952s are gorgeous cards with the printed autographs of the players in a panel where their names were printed. It's extremely expensive in top shape—$50,000-plus was the figure most often quoted during the writing of this book. I'd rather recommend an alternative. Buy individual 1952 star cards: the Mantle, Robinson, Campanella, Reese, Berra, Ford, and Mays.

The three sets from 1966 through 1968 are all good buys. I like the 1963 sets because they contain the Stargell and Rose rookies, but I'd avoid the 1964 set because there are no great first-year-player cards. Stay away from the 1962 set with the brown borders, even though it has Gaylord Perry's rookie card. This set is never good enough for collectors, and it's quite ugly. It hasn't really improved aesthetically over time the way some other profoundly ugly cards do. It will increase modestly, I think, but it will never have great investment value. Perry finally did get elected to the HOF in 1990, but his enshrinement barely nudged the value of his card. The Roger Maris card from that season is still worth considerably more, almost double the Perry card, and there's virtually no chance that Maris will be voted in unless the Veteran's Committee goes soft.

There is a dramatic drop-off in price in the 1973 and 1974 sets, mainly because 1973 was the last year Topps printed and distributed cards in series. Most years before 1973 are good buys, but you should probably stay away from the 1970 and 1971 sets. The 1971s have black borders which are easily scratched; they're not particularly attractive, and I'm not high on them in terms of investment value. The 1970s have no rookie cards that drive the price up (the third-year Ryan is the most expensive card).

I'm not particularly fond of the 1956 or 1960 sets, because in those years Topps pictured the players horizontally, a pose I feel isn't attractive except on very old cards where playing field scenes were depicted. Also, neither of those sets has rookie cards with big upside potential.

I think the 1953 set is way overpriced, and overvalued by collectors. They contain red and black bottoms, and they suffer the same condition rarity the 1971s do, except worse. They're frequently fudged, so be careful if you buy the Mantle or Mays card, the key cards in the set. People take Magic Markers or crayons and touch up the borders, hoping to up the tough cards a half-grade or so. Because it's almost impossible to acquire a near mint or mint set of 1953s, they're expensive and unreasonably so.

Are there any good buys in the Topps sets issued from 1980 through 1989? Yes, but a qualified yes, because you're crapshooting with current stars (some already proven over several seasons, so the bets are not so risky). I'm cautiously bullish on the 1980 and the 1983, because the 1980 has the Rickey Henderson rookie card, and the 1983 has the Sandberg, Gwynn, and Boggs rookies. The 1985 set has speculative potential, only because there are so many good (not yet great) first-year Topps cards: Puckett, McGwire's Olympic team card, Clemens, and Eric Davis. In 1990 you could have purchased a pair of sets each of the 1980, 1983, and 1985 issues for about $750. Or you could have taken the $750 and bought a single 1975 set, which has the Brett and Yount rookie cards.

Faced with the decision, the 1975 is a more conservative investment. The other three sets are riskier, but they have a tremendous upside if the cards of the eight players mentioned begin to take off. Sandberg's and Henderson's cards already escalated sharply during the 1990 season.

You already know how I feel about active players, so if you are a young and frisky investor-cum-speculator, remember that I reminded you more than once to be very careful. (I don't want to sound mean-spirited, but a competitive book on cards, collectibles, and investments published in 1989 recommended, "Greenwell—the next Yaz. Buy." To be fair, the book did, however, make a buy recommendation on Rickey Henderson, a far better tout and one that paid off handsomely.)

If you're starting with less than $1,000, obviously you won't be able to afford a vintage Topps set. What should you do? Buy sets of all the companies (Donruss, Fleer, Topps, Score, and Upper Deck) from 1986 to 1991, with the exception being the 1986 Donruss set. In that five-year period, you'll be able to afford several sets, so you must patiently shop for the best prices. Buy them "factory-unopened," and let them mature in your closet. When the superstars emerge in the late 1990s or early in the next century, you'll be sure to own their rookie cards.

A riskier approach would be to pick a company and a year where you think there is potential. Then try to procure 70 or 80 sets at $15 to $18, or as close to wholesale as you can find. This will require a substantial amount of phone calling and research in the trade press.

In addition to the Topps sets I mentioned earlier that were not very good buys, I'd also like to present a list of items that you should avoid. It's something to muse over until you are comfortable enough in the market to know what to pass on without expert advice.

1. The 1984 and 1986 Donruss sets. In 1990, the 1984 set was trading in the $250 to $325 range at the beginning of the

summer. Extremely volatile, by midseason the price had soft-
ened because of a single piece of downer news. Don Mattingly
had to miss almost the entire second half of the season because
of his nagging back injury. This set is unreasonably high
because of the Mattingly rookie card, and I can't see it
recovering to new heights, especially since Mattingly's career is
in jeopardy. (Yes, he did return with a flourish in September,
but back injuries can be long-term.) I'm more bullish on Jose
Canseco, but the 1986 set is much too high because of his
rookie card. If he has had back surgery by the time you read
this, uh-oh.

2. O-Pee-Chee (or "OPC") cards. These are the Canadian
counterparts to Topps cards, and they were issued beginning in
1965. They were printed in smaller quantities than Topps and
so they're scarcer, but that doesn't make them spectacular
buys. They usually look exactly like the Topps cards except for
the words "Printed in Canada" on the reverse. Sometimes all
the reverse type is in French. Collectors have a strange
fascination with O-Pee-Chees, and I've always wondered why.
They do not appreciate as fast as American cards, except
perhaps in Montreal and Toronto.

3. 1948–55 Bowman cards. There's nothing particularly
wrong with these cards; in fact, they are quite striking and
beautiful except for the 1955s, which feature the TV set design.
Bowman was the only game in town between 1948 and 1951,
and the sets are high-priced. But they appear to be in a bit of a
stall. They're difficult to move from the dealer's point of view
(demand has slowed), so I can't recommend them. Topps
issued a Bowman set in 1989, and it's too early to predict
whether it'll be a collector's item in the next century.

4. "Error" cards of any kind, except the T-206 "Magie," which
you probably wouldn't be able to find even if you could afford
it. Do not get sucked onto the error card merry-go-round. After
you've walked enough shows, some guy will approach you and

show you 50 cards without printing on the reverse, or Billy Ripken's card with the obscenity on the bat, or some weird delineation of a properly printed card. Don't buy any of them. There are collectors who thrive on errors, and they're not going to make money. There are many reasons. There are too many errors every season to focus on. Once errors are publicized heavily, they usually become suddenly and widely available, so nobody has any real idea about what they're realistically worth.

The Sherry Magee card in the T-206 series is special. Magee was a lifetime .291 hitter, more than respectable by today's standards. Twentieth Century Tobacco originally misspelled his name with an "i," but the error was quickly corrected. Very few cards were actually printed and released. The error card lists for more than $7,000, while Sherry's correctly spelled name is worth about $50.

5. "Traded," "update," "glossy," or any Tiffany, gimmick, or "limited edition" sets of almost any kind. My feeling is that these marketing ploys by the card companies are bad buys. You will never feel you know the straight dope on just how many were issued. Updated and traded sets merely exist to correct missed calls by the card companies. The traded sets exist because player movement from team to team is much more frequent today than in the past. Since they must issue their full set print orders well before the next season's rosters are known, they do a lot of guessing. And they guess wrong a lot. Unless special rookie cards are in some update sets—the 1984 Fleer Update is one such exception, because it has Clemens', Gooden's, and Puckett's first cards—I'd avoid them.

6. Perez-Steel cards. These oversized cards are recent issues and popular among collectors, because they lend themselves to autographs. But the prices have gone to ridiculous levels considering there's nothing vintage about them. The other tip-off may be that Beckett doesn't list them in either his collectibles or his card price guides. Stay away.

7. Players near the end of their careers who are borderline candidates for the HOF. These are the guys you spend hours arguing about over beers. You know who they are, and they've had a few—or even several—great seasons, but they're not clear-cut choices. Their careers have peaked, or are in solid decline, or already over. You've marveled at their grace, admired their heroics, remembered their key game-winning hits, and they've had a profound effect on how you view a player's talent. Perhaps you'd like very much for them to someday be on enough of those sportswriters' ballots. Forget it. You cannot wish a player in the HOF. I'd like to remind you who these players are, just in case you've forgotten.

> Dwight Evans
> Eddie Murray
> Andre Dawson
> Dale Murphy
> Dave Parker
> Jim Rice
> Fred Lynn
> Gary Carter
> Keith Hernandez
> Steve Garvey

By the way, I'm not in any way inferring that I don't think any of these guys should get in. I could probably make a better case for Parker, Evans, and Murray than most fans, in fact.

The following I'd call "borderline positive," meaning they have a better shot than the 10 players on the above list but are not 50 percent chance or better by any means.

> Alan Trammell
> Bert Blyleven
> Tony Perez
> Ozzie Smith
> Dave Winfield
> Rollie Fingers

I realize by the time you buy this book, Rollie Fingers may already have been elected, since the winter of 1990 was his first year of eligibility. I'm being conservative here, because even though he's number one on the all-time saves list, relief pitchers (except for Hoyt Wilhelm) haven't been put onto too many HOF ballots yet.

There are two other pitchers who are probable-to-certain HOFers whom I haven't mentioned in earlier chapters. The reason is that they're pitchers with more than 300 wins, and their election will certainly boost the price of their memorabilia and autographs. But their cards will not increase that dramatically because they're pitchers.

They are Phil Niekro and Don Sutton.

HOW TO SELL
WHAT YOU BOUGHT

The question I hear most when I'm at my table at card shows should be apparent by now.

"Is this a good time to sell my cards, Mr. Rosen?"

Here is my stock reply, more or less.

"Well, Mr. _____, I can't answer that. What you're asking me, really, is if I think the market is at its peak and about to begin a reversal. I'm not sure. I know what these cards are worth right this instant. Today. Not yesterday, not tomorrow, but now. I would be less than honest if I recommended your selling them to me now. Of course, I'd rather you dispose of your collection with me instead of my competitor at the next table. But I'd also be less than honest if I suggested you wait a few months because they're certain to be worth even more.

"When to sell doesn't usually matter with me or any competent dealer. Remember, since I'm not a collector, I have to keep the merchandise and money constantly in motion. My profit is simply a function of time. Since I'm willing to take less profit than the other guy, I'm continually aware of little dips and surges. And because I do this every waking hour, I have a distinct advantage over the part-time investor or collector.

"I don't know what the market will be like next week, let alone next month or next year, and neither does anybody else. If it goes up, I pay more for good stuff. If it goes down, or even if it collapses, it just means I'll pay less and sell it for a smaller profit. I don't predict these things, and neither should you.

"The answers to the critical questions, 'Should I cash in my chips now? Do I need the money?' have to come from you. If all you ever do is wonder whether the market has reached its peak—and aren't hard-pressed for cash—you'll probably not sell. You may not ever sell. You may give them to your grandchildren. And that's okay, too."

I do not say the following:

Many baseball hobbyists are eccentric in that they don't want to sell their collections—they merely *think* they want to. So they practice shopping it around in order to make themselves feel better. It's sort of a neurosis. They're constantly checking their assets, reminding themselves the cards are worth hard currency. It's a strange affliction, but having seen grown men moved to tears when they're selling their cards, I've learned to spot the pretenders. My instinct is so honed that I usually can type these folks before they reach my table.

The conclusion of my little spiel:

"If you ask for my—or any other dealer's—opinion about where the market is headed, you're setting yourself up for a loaded answer. Sure, I want your cards, and I'll pay you a fair price. If I want them badly enough, I'll pay top dollar, more than the guy down the aisle. So here's my offer. It's a onetime offer, and I may not feel this way tomorrow. Most people want to shop around for their best price, and that's fine. But then they come back and say, 'Another dealer is willing to top it. Can you go higher than he can?' When I'm buying, I don't prefer to play the auction game. In fact, if you're willing to wait for my next auction, you can find out what the market value really is. Meanwhile, take your time and decide. I'll be here all day."

Now that I've said that, remember, dealers are hungry for your good cards and memorabilia. They want them badly; and they want them today, because there isn't that much wonderful material available. If we dealers don't buy, we have nothing to sell. A good dealer likes action. He's often bought and resold the same high-quality items several times over a period of years.

It is probably better to sell your collection during the heat of the baseball season than it is during the off-season. This is when top-shelf dealers tend to get antsy, especially if there's a lack of product, and they may be willing to make a better-than-usual deal. There seem to be more shows in the summer than any other season, and this is the time when people who have forgotten the pleasure of the game decide they want to collect anew. A great many hobbyists are born again between Memorial Day and Labor Day. But this is just the way it seems. There's no hard evidence that cards bring higher prices in July rather than some other month. I've seen the market active in the winter when baseball doesn't seem to be on the minds of most collectors.

MR. MINT'S MAXIM: *If you are liquidating an entire collection, it's usually better to do business only with a dealer who is willing to make an offer on the entire collection. If a dealer is at all hesitant or whines in any way when negotiating with you, he's consciously or subconsciously discrediting some of your goods. His objective is to get you to take less money than you might be able to get.*

I'm always out-front about this. If a collector wants to sell his collection, I'll buy the dreck, too. I will break down the items if asked, and then I'll be blunt (some might call it brutally honest) if I see things I have absolutely no interest in or can't possibly sell on my best day. A smart dealer won't want to risk offending a customer by saying he doesn't want a particular junky item (that the seller might think is great) among a cache of gems. Why scotch a deal by insulting someone's taste? I often pass on collections because the seller either wants too much or I don't like the condition. But it that's the case, I won't even make an offer, even if the seller asks.

Another question I'm often asked is whether it's better to dispose of an extensive collection piecemeal or all in one shot. You may indeed do better overall if you shop certain types of material to dealers who specialize in what you're offering. There's always someone who buys tough series commons, and there's always someone who'll buy star cards, and there are dealers out there who only want to be involved with rookies. But bear this in mind: It takes more time to sell a collection in little chunks. It's not easy to apply the regional theory when selling a lot of diversified material (McCovey in San Francisco, Stargell in Pittsburgh, Hodges in Brooklyn, and so forth). What you gain in cash may be given up in time and aggravation, postage and insurance. Weigh the pluses and minuses. Obviously, if you have a business trip or vacation already scheduled for some part of the country where your cards may have more momentum on the selling market, then it's to your advantage to break off that particular chunk and tote them along. (If you are selling a gonzo collection for a lot of money, you should expect the top dealers to travel to you. But then they'll want to make a deal for the entire lot, or at least a major portion.)

If you're selling a very expensive item or collection, it might pay for you to get a professional appraisal from a reputable dealer. Even if you're not selling, it might be a good idea to get a substantial collection appraised for insurance purposes. Many underwriters require it, and since most people don't keep their collections in bank vaults or safes, there's more than a nominal risk of loss. Usually, a formal appraisal costs money. I charge 2 percent of the estimated value. Some dealers might charge 5 percent or work on a set fee arrangement, depending on how long it will take. A good appraiser should be knowledgeable, have references (I can provide a well-known auction house when I'm asked), and make a detailed description of the cards and goods, the amounts, and the date of appraisal. I use my letterhead, and offer additional assurance of my opinion. I'm confident enough to buy the collection for the amount I appraise it.

MR. MINT'S MAXIM: *The baseball card and memorabilia business, unlike others, does not have people who do nothing but appraise goods. Appraisers are dealers like myself. Do not use an appraiser who is not willing to outright buy your cards at his appraised price. Someone who is willing to evaluate your collection in a given price range and is not willing to offer at least the low end is not giving you an honest opinion.*

Other than shopping your cards at a good-sized show, there are a few other methods of disposal you can use. You can take your cards to the local card shop, but unless the proprietor is doing a large volume (and most do not), you will not get a fair market offer. By fair market, I mean 60 to 70 percent (higher on gem mint) of the book value of pre-1976 cards. Most card shops cannot afford to work on small margins. If you get an offer from a card shop, you might ask him what his sell price would be on the same set or item. If he's hesitant ("I can't really say unless I see a specific set"), or quotes a price that indicates an unusually large gap, then you're in the wrong place.

When a dealer is negotiating with you on cards or any items listed in a price guide, do not be shy about asking how he arrived at his offer. If he doesn't pull out a reference, you should ask which guide book he's using. Then find out what percent of book he's offering.

For instance, say a collector wants to sell a Turkey Red Walter Johnson #99. It's a rare card, and the condition is dead on the borderline between two columns in the price guide. It's an excellent card, and the Beckett's lists two prices, "EX-MT" and "VG-EX," and the respective prices are $1,350 and $650. I'll use $1,000 as the sell price. If I offer $600, I'll tell the seller that I'm offering only 60 percent because off-condition cards do not sell well. I may ask only $700 on resale, and I'll disclose this, too. I would also say that if I were certain I could find a buyer reasonably quickly at $900 or $1,000, then I could offer $700 or $800. If the seller still looks cross-eyed or confused in any way (he has heard of my reputation for paying top prices, right?), then I also explain that if it was a perfect Johnson card—among the best I'd ever seen—I would have offered $1,350 because I'd easily be able to ask, and get, $1,500 or $1,600 for it.

My sermonette here is, information should be free. It's the advice that costs, and I'm afraid it's not worth what you pay for it much of the time. I'm never afraid to reveal my plans, and neither should any other dealer.

MR. MINT'S MAXIM: *Try to do your selling to what I call an action dealer, a guy who is a businessman first, and a card lover second. How can you tell? He is the guy who sold you a rare card or very nice set just a few months ago and calls you to buy it back at a profit.*

You can also sell cards to your friends, which is how the hobby started becoming a business (it was simple swapping in the old days; cash exchanges were rare and considered déclassé among connoisseurs). But now that substantial sums are frequently involved, I want to caution you against cashing in with your buddy (who promised to top any dealer buy offer). Your heart is in the right place, and so is his. You would rather sell them to someone you know will give the cards a nice home instead of the impersonal dealer who is going to immediately resell them.

But your friend is thinking investment (no matter what he says), because even though you're giving him a bargain, he may be wondering what they'll be worth next month. If he's tempted to try and flip them for a relatively rapid resale and finds out the offer is skimpy, you may end up losing a friend. When the stakes get high enough, the poker game is no longer friendly. It's serious. That's why shrewd, professional dealers are personable rather than personal. (Remember, one reason why banks exist is so you don't have to ask for a loan from your friends or relatives. You may pay more interest at the bank, but in the long run it's far cheaper emotionally.)

The only other place to sell your cards is on the auction block. But you will have more things to worry about, and you will wait longer for the total payment on your lots. Remember, too, that if you're attached emotionally to your cards (something I've warned you against earlier in this book), you will have to give them up for two months or more before they're sold. Auction houses need a long lead time to plan their sales and fill their lot openings. However, with several people bidding on your goods, there is a greater chance to reap higher amounts than a dealer might pay. (Some auction houses are willing to advance a portion of the low estimate or reserve bid to sellers. It's a consideration if you're in need of cash.) Just as you must know the bidder's rules for buying, you should be well versed with the consignment policy. I charge 10 percent of the hammer price. Buyers pay no premium. Should you sell a set of cards through me for $1,500, I would send you a check for $1,350 as soon as the sale was over.

Timing differs on the transfer of funds, and you'll have to read the fine print of the various consignment agreements before you send your material. Some houses pay within a set number of days after the sale, while others will not send payment until after they've received a check from the winning bidder. Most reputable houses do not release the lots to winning bidders until funds have cleared the bank. Once you enter into an agreement with an auction gallery, and your goods are safely delivered, then the responsibility rests on its shoulders.

Choosing an auction house is more than finding the best deal or the one that advertises its sales the most (though these are important factors). You must find an agent you feel comfortable with and trust. Obviously, if he's any good at all, he'll want to bring you high prices (and thus, high commissions for himself); otherwise he won't get any repeat business. If he's confident that a certain lot you're selling will bring a high price, he won't try and talk you into lowering the reserve bid. Conversely, he will tell you if he thinks your reserve is too low. Some will not. There is nothing to stop an auctioneer who also is a dealer from buying an item for his own inventory. Know in advance if there is a seller's penalty (usually a fixed fee or small percentage) for lots that fail to sell. Know, too, what other fees you must pay, if any, such as return shipping and insurance.

If you decide to ship your cards and goods off to a dealer or auction house, remember that they must be carefully packed and insured against damage. If you're sending several boxes of cards, make sure you place them in a larger box with newspaper, foam padding, or bubble wrap. Whether you're sending via UPS, Federal Express, or the U.S. Postal System, you cannot overprotect baseball cards.

CARING FOR YOUR CARDS
AND PRECIOUS COLLECTIBLES

Let's assume you're going to accumulate a lot of cards and assorted baseball antiquities. Let's assume also that you'll want to hold on to at least some of your collection for a substantial period of time. Since cards tend to be fragile, you must take the utmost care to protect them, especially very old, expensive cards. If you just bought a card for $1,000, your instinct would be to treat it at least as well as a fine piece of jewelry, and you'd be right. If your collection is running into a reasonably large amount of money, get it insured (and reappraised every two years or even more frequently).

If you own very expensive small items, such as press pins, and you expect to keep them for some time, my suggestion is to place them in a bank safety-deposit box, rather than leave them casually in your dresser drawer. They're precisely the kind of items that even moronic burglars will steal before they get to your stereo and TV set. They will not know what they're worth, but they'll know that they're valuable jewelry. A small safe in a walk-in closet isn't a bad idea either.

When I collected, my cards began to dislocate all the clothes in my bedroom closet. Out went the shirts and trousers, and in went the boxes of Topps and Bowmans. I was so paranoid about harming them that a downstairs closet was unacceptable. They had to be stored upstairs. I live in Bergen County in New Jersey, and this is one of the top flood zones in the nation. What if there was a flood? My cards would be ruined. You don't need to be overzealous about this, just sensible.

MR. MINT'S MAXIM: *Never has the advice "Store in a cool, dry place" been more apt than as it applies to baseball cards. Do not leave them in a hot attic, and do not keep them in a damp basement. Cards, especially those with gum, can stick and lose their gloss in excessive heat. Daunting as it might seem, find yourself an empty closet, or build another set of bookshelves in your den or living room.*

If you find yourself accumulating loose cards, make sure the valuable ones are kept apart in single-card plastic holders. They come in all kinds of thicknesses, from very inexpensive polyethylene (like Baggies material) to semi-rigid and rigid. Most of the semi-rigid holders are fine, but you must gingerly take the card in and out of the holder. It's easier to damage a corner than with the screw-down Lucite holders.

The screw-down Lucite holders are the preferred storage method for cards worth several hundred dollars and more. They take all the wear and scratches that a card might get. They accommodate small-format tobacco cards to anything manu-factured today (except Exhibits, Turkey Reds, and other over-sized cards). Collectors love these things, but some dealers, myself included, find they're not worth the trouble. The main drawback to screw-down holders is that it's a terrible imposition when you want to sell it, because any serious buyer is going to want you to remove it. If I wanted to spend my time with a screwdriver, I'd have become a cabinetmaker, not a card dealer. The snap-shut plastic holders are relatively new. You might find they're an excellent compromise between slip-ins and screw-downs.

Less valuable cards can be stored two ways, in boxes or display sheets. If you're more collector than investor and obsessed with your newly bought booty, you might feel the need to look at your cards frequently. Then I recommend you buy albums and put all the cards in the loose-leaf binders.

MR. MINT'S MAXIM: *Use only top-loading binder sheets. Do not buy the side-loading sheets. As you turn the pages on a side-load sheet, the tips and corners of the cards have stress. On a top-load sheet, this doesn't occur. Also side loaders aren't as practical, because the cards tend to slip out when you're carrying them. Loose-leaf binders are best stored upright, just like a book in a bookshelf.*

One other word of caution on plastic sheets. Make sure you buy sheets without PVC, polyvinylchloride, the plastic preservative. If they're accidentally exposed to heat for even a short period, the cards will stick. The best-case scenario then is that they'll only lose their gloss. The worst case is that you'll sear the face of the cards when you try to remove them.

Far more convenient for storage, but not as practical for viewing, is the standard 800-count box so commonly seen in stores and at shows. (Never buy a box where the closing flaps fold on the inside. They're not that common anymore, but if you use them, it's a big mistake. Inside flaps can crumple the edges of the cards.) With a small wad of tissue paper, the 800-count boxes conveniently hold a complete set of 792 Topps cards, or complete sets from the other manufacturers. When you're carrying them, you'll hear slight movement. But they won't shift in any alarming way. They fit snugly and the wiggle is acceptable, so long as you don't handle them like a cocktail shaker. If they were any tighter, you'd damage them when you put them in or removed them. As it is, it takes a fair amount of practice to quickly get them in and out without dinging the edges. You can also store a 660-count Donruss or Fleer set in an 800-count box, or a smaller one, so long as you keep enough tissue paper in it to keep them from jostling. The older sets came in smaller issues, so they don't fill up the boxes. Just use a lot more tissue paper.

When I was collecting, I used cotton to fill the dead space, because it was softer. But I was a lunatic about this. If I had a set of 1975 Topps minis, for example, I just pushed them all the way to one end and used cotton on the sides so the cards couldn't move front to front or side to side.

MR. MINT'S MAXIM: *When you're storing your cards in a box, remember that no movement means no wear.*

If you're accumulating bats, remember to keep them in individual bat holders. Today, there are several wall-mount display pieces, usually manufactured in Lucite or other hard plastic. If you're transporting them to and from shows to add an elusive autograph, you should always put a tube-type athletic sock (the cheap nylon ones will do fine) around the barrel to avoid getting it scratched in the car trunk. Don't leave them clattering together in a duffel bag as if you're on your way to a Sunday morning softball game.

Baseballs need care, too. There are basically two kinds of ball holders: the spherical type with gilt-colored plastic base and the heavier Lucite cubes. The sphericals are more convenient, because they're easier to open when you want to inspect the ball. The cubes, which look far classier (and are more expensive), are cumbersome to open and close. There's a new type of cube with a walnut base with optically clear plastic that you might consider. The manufacturer claims that it blocks the sun's harmful ultraviolet rays. But even if you use it, I don't think you should ever leave a valuable, autographed ball in the sunlight. I'm now marketing a very expensive ball holder that retails for $22. Obviously, I'm not expecting anyone to buy them for Robin Roberts' or Bob Feller's signature balls.

I've recently heard that many collectors are using clear-finish Krylon spray coating to protect balls. They swear that with Krylon a ball will never yellow, a signature will never fade. But nobody really knows. No matter how safe someone insists it is, I wouldn't use any kind of spray, even if someone put a gun to my head.

MR. MINT'S MAXIM: *Altering a collectible in any way, even minutely, is a risk to its future value.*

Programs and literature, and any old paper collectibles, should be stored in plastic holders. Rare books should have plastic "dust jackets" to protect the covers. Store as much of this as you can in an upright position, preferably on a bookshelf. Don't stack everything casually. The pages will have less chance of sticking on the one day your air conditioner breaks down or there's a power failure on an overly humid day.

Old newspapers should be kept out of sunlight or they will yellow. If you frame them, use acid-free mounting. A professional framer or art supply store can check a frame of any recent acquisition and help you choose safe materials.

You'll find all sorts of display pieces for almost any collectible item in the pages of SCD and the other trades. So it's unsurprising to discover there are Lucite boxes made especially for fielder's gloves, too. There's a plethora of products for hobbyists, and I've always found that if I have to improvise, a well-stocked stationery store will have something useful to house a collectible. But this part of the business is becoming more technical all the time, and the best place to keep up with it is in the trade papers.

CLOSING SERMONS

By now you may be reeling just a little from the deluge of information about baseball cards and collectibles. Yes, I admit it. There's a lot to know. One of the great attractions about this business is that I learn something new or make a fresh discovery every day. I've made it a point to stay ahead of my competitors by accruing more knowledge and working harder. I guarantee that if you immerse yourself—in the literature and at the weekend shows—you'll begin to feel comfortable after three months, confident after six months, and even smug about your investing capabilities after only a year.

Remember, it is not that difficult, and most other folks in the game will not spend even the minimum amount of time to really learn what they need to know. They're headstrong, and they let things like childish team loyalties cloud what would be otherwise sound judgment. Yes, I'm still a diehard Yankee fan. But I never let this fact affect me on a business deal. No, I'm not particularly fond of the other New York franchise, but I won't kick sand in the face of someone who wants to make a deal involving Mets memorabilia.

As I finished writing this book, I made a trip to Anchorage,

Alaska, where I bought $100,000 worth of baseball cards. I've been to several places in the United States on buying trips, but I'd never been that far away. It was cold up there, and I hate being in the cold. Why couldn't the cards be in Honolulu? I wondered. (Because they weren't, that's why.) But I made $21,000 in three days, and that, folks, is what makes that kind of a trek worthwhile.

On the flight home, I wondered what kind of lessons I could draw from the trip that might be useful for my readers. There were two, and I covered them in the book, but I'd like to remind you of them.

First, I'm willing to drag my body to places where nobody else will. This is nothing but common sense. Sure, there were plenty of dealers in Los Angeles, San Francisco, and Seattle who could have traveled to Anchorage—and it's a lot less taxing trip for them—but I was the one who was willing to do it.

Second, I made 21 percent on my investment (gross profit) in three days. Subtracting my expenses (travel, advertising, and other overhead), the net profit is somewhat less. I'm willing to work on a small margin as long as I don't have to keep the merchandise in my safe for too long. Fast turnover is everything, and this is no secret, but you'd be surprised how many dealers and investors have trouble grasping this basic concept. I have on occasion laid out $150,000 to make even less (only $10,000).

Don't be fearful of selling what you just bought when a buyer comes along at the "right" or "fair" price. Do not get caught up in the syndrome where when somebody offers you what amounts to a profit for an item, you immediately wonder what it will be worth if you hold on to it for a longer period of time. Only if you truly love an object should you keep it.

Once you make an honest profit, the feeling is intoxicating. I know a guy who's been collecting bats for only six months. He wasn't pressed to sell anything, but the first time another collector admired a signed Willie McCovey store bat in his apartment, the visitor wondered whether he'd part with it. The bat's owner found himself saying, "It's yours for $225." When he first bought it, he remembered how much he admired McCovey when he played for the Giants. It was a great memento. He'd paid $150 for the bat just two months before. Now, $75 isn't a substantial amount of money for this fellow. He spends more than that on dinner for two at a nice restaurant. But because he's a retailer and is also very practical, he looked at the transaction this way: *I made a 50 percent profit in two months.* There is no other financial instrument that could have given him that rate of return so quickly. He told me that he'd miss the McCovey stick, naturally, but he could always find another one. And besides, the positive feeling of turning a profit overcame the negative feeling of parting with a collectible.

Now, of course, he's smart enough to know that he can't do that sort of deal every minute—it did kind of fall in his lap, after all. But can you imagine if he assumed a more aggressive posture? Suppose he took a booth at a small show for $75 or $100 and brought along two dozen bats. Or suppose he buys a small display ad in *Sports Collectors Digest*? Yes, in order to make a return on your investment, you must sell. If you sell, you're vaguely becoming a dealer; just realize there's nothing vulgar about it.

One final concept I want to make sure you understand is that it's always better to buy one spectacular old item than a bunch of lower demand, lesser quality pieces for the same price. A singles investor won't do as well as the home run, swing-for-the-fence kind of guy who's willing to take the occasional big cut at the plate. My early, big risks were with borrowed cash, an idea that made me more than a bit nervous. While I'm not suggesting you mortgage your house to buy up a collection, I am saying this: Once you're confident, you should make the kind of move that gets your adrenaline pumping. The downside—what if I have to sell what I just bought at a loss?—should be calculable. And you should be able to absorb a perceived loss (not being able to unload what you bought for a period of time, or selling it for the same price months later—which is a real dollar loss even if inflation is minimal).

The upside should be a modest to a handsome profit. Hope for handsome, and plan to settle for modest.

MR. MINT'S FINAL MAXIMS:

1. *Don't get emotionally involved with an object you're negotiating to buy.*
2. *Learn how to properly grade a card before you buy an expensive one.*
3. *Condition, condition, condition. Don't buy cards in off condition unless they're very scarce.*
4. *Don't buy any collectible when you're the least bit unsure of its authenticity.*
5. *Buy items of famous Hall of Famers, preferably deceased.*
6. *Don't play the commodities game. Invest, don't gamble. Avoid current rookie speculation.*

If this is the first book on cards you've bought, you should begin immediately building a reference library. Some suggestions are included in the appendix that follows this chapter.

Good hunting, and remember the Mint Man when you begin building your portfolio of cards and collectibles. I hope to see you at a baseball card show sometime soon. (If you'd like to comment on this book, please write to me at 70 I Chestnut Ridge Rd., Montvale, NJ 07645.)

APPENDIX

——

SUGGESTED REFERENCES

Following is a list of periodicals and books that I keep for handy reference. I highly recommend them to anyone who wants to become seriously involved in learning more about the basic investment tenets outlined in this book. There are some investment newsletters and tout sheets, published mostly by dealers who are interested in selling their wares. While there's nothing objectionable about that, I haven't yet read one I'd recommend.

PERIODICALS

Sports Collectors Digest (Krause Publications, Inc., 700 E. State St., Iola, WI 54990). A weekly trade newspaper for hobbyists, collectors, investors, and dealers, it is considered the single indispensable authority on cards and collectibles. The price guide is probably as close to being up-to-date as anything you'll find in print. Single copy, $3.25, available in many card shops. One-year subscription, $39.95. Save your back copies.

Beckett's Baseball Card Monthly (4887 Alpha Rd., Ste. 200, Dallas, TX 75244). Read this to find out what Dr. Jim Beckett is thinking, but be aware that price guide information is three months old. Single copy, $2.50. One-year subscription, $19.95.

Current Card Prices (P.O. Box 480, Islip, NY 11730). Monthly price guide for most cards, 1948 to present, on newsprint. Single copy, $2.50, available in many card shops. One-year subscription, $21.95.

BOOKS

Baseball Encyclopedia (Macmillan), 8th edition, $49.95. Contains the name and complete record of anyone who ever played an inning (or part of one) or made a plate appearance in professional baseball. New edition has information on Negro-leagues players.

Sports Encyclopedia of Baseball (St. Martin's Press), 1989 edition, by David S. Neft and Richard M. Cohen. Among many valuable statistics, it gives complete team rosters and details on All-Star games and postseason play. An important reference tool if you're collecting autographed team baseballs.

Baseball Card Dealer Directory (Meckler Books). Nationwide listings of places to buy and sell cards.

Baseball History—An Annual of Original Baseball Research (Meckler Books). An interesting compilation of statistics and history, good shopping terrain for collecting ideas.

The Sports Collectors Bible (Wallace-Homestead Book Co., Box B1, Des Moine, IA 50304), by Bert Sugar. The first good guide, and although it's 16 years old, it led the way in identifying specialties that were in demand by collectors. Ignore the price guide information.

Topps Baseball Cards—The Complete Picture Collection (Warner Books). Published in 1989, it's a 40-year history of the most famous card company.

Classic Baseball Cards—The Golden Years 1886–1956 (Warner Books). A picture book by Frank Slocum which complements the Topps book. Illustrates what the very old cards looked like in mint condition.

Sports Collectors Digest Baseball Card Price Guide (Warner Books). A comprehensive annual guide to rough prices of modern cards.

The Sport Americana Baseball Card Price Guide (Edgewater), by Dr. James Beckett, $14.95. The other major annual authority that competes with the SCD version above.

The Sport Americana Price Guide to Baseball Collectibles (Edgewater), by Dr. James Beckett, $12.95. Canadian cards, doodads, stickers, and esoteric issues. The most useful price information is on press pins.

The Sport Americana Baseball Card Alphabetical Checklist #4 (Edgewater), by Dr. James Beckett. Useful tool for looking up players' cards and determining complete sets; lists variations.

Official 1948–1989/90 Baseball Card Alphabetical Cross-reference Guide (Martin-Smith), by John F. Remark and Nathan M. Bisk. Good reference source for looking up first-year cards on players.

Baseball Autograph Handbook (Krause Publications), by Mark Allen Baker, $19.95. Features specimen signatures of Hall of Famers, and price information (though outdated).